Implementing Cost-Effective Assistive Computer Technology

A How-To-Do-It Manual for Librarians®

Jane Vincent

HOW-TO-DO-IT MANUALS®

NUMBER 181

Neal-Schuman Publishers, Inc.

New York   London

> ► Companion Blog

Don't miss this book's companion blog:

To access links to and information about new and useful accessibility programs and apps, changes in legislation, innovations in the assistive technology field, and other parallel topics, go to:

http://www.janevincent.com/iceact

Published by Neal-Schuman Publishers, Inc.
100 William St., Suite 2004
New York, NY 10038
http://www.neal-schuman.com

Printed and bound in the United States of America.

The paper used in this publication meets the minimum requirements of American National Standard for Information Sciences—Permanence of Paper for Printed Library Materials, ANSI Z39.48-1992.

Library of Congress Cataloging-in-Publication Data

Vincent, Jane.
    Implementing cost-effective assistive computer technology : a how-to-do-it manual for librarians / Jane Vincent.
        p. cm. — (How-to-do-it manuals ; no. 181)
    Includes bibliographical references and index.
    ISBN 978-1-55570-762-0 (alk. paper)
    1. Libraries and people with disabilities—United States. 2. Self-help devices for people with disabilities—United States. I. Title.

Z711.92.H3V56 2012
027.6'63—dc23
                             2011033985

For James Edward Knox
and
Laurence Minsky

Contents

List of Checklists, Templates, and Worksheets

Foreword

I was honored when Jane asked me to write a foreword for her book *Implementing Cost-Effective Assistive Computer Technology*. I had no qualms about introducing the book as I have observed her work with many libraries in the San Francisco Bay Area, I recommend her to clients, and I bring my assistive technology questions to her as well. But I was a bit puzzled as to what I could contribute to the book. After looking at numerous other forewords, it seemed clear that I should answer two basic questions: why the library community needs this book and why Jane Vincent is the author to read.

Since 1975 my own career has involved helping libraries improve their services to people with disabilities. At that time, most libraries sent anyone with a disability, or a patron acting on behalf of someone with a disability, to the nearest regional library of the National Library Service for the Blind and Physically Handicapped and considered that they'd done their job. Any professional discussions on the topic centered on serving either blind people and people with visual impairments or Deaf people and people with hearing impairments. A few progressive libraries provided large type books, braille signage, commercial talking books, TTYs, and signed story hours.

In 1990, the passage of landmark civil rights legislation known as the Americans with Disabilities Act (ADA) compelled reluctant libraries to consider that everything in and about their libraries should be considered from the perspective of people with disabilities—and disabilities other than visual and hearing ones. Building accessibility was the first priority for most libraries. But once libraries could focus beyond entrance ramps, stack aisle widths, and accessible bathrooms, they turned their attention to assistive technologies, including computers.

The American Library Association (ALA) immediately began providing assistance (through publications and conference programs) to help libraries address the ADA. The federal government offered aid through Library Services and Technology Act (LSTA) grant money, which funded many pilot projects across the country. The outcomes of many of these programs demonstrated common preconceptions and problems for libraries.

One of the proudest moments in my life as a librarian was in 2001, when ALA—after Council defeated the measure in 2000—finally passed a policy on serving people with disabilities that looked beyond compliance with laws and regulations to equal access in the broadest sense. I was fortunate to serve as editor and chief lobbyist for this "controversial" policy, drafted and sponsored by the ADA Assembly (now the Accessibility Assembly). The Accessibility Policy gave libraries a tool other than the ADA to bolster their arguments—and budget request rationales—for new services and technologies to recalcitrant library boards and local governments.

Despite all this technical, financial, and policy assistance, many libraries still cling to the initial arguments and issues around providing adaptive technologies that they presented 20 years ago. Their contentions have remained surprisingly—and depressingly—constant, no matter what the latest technologies are or where the libraries are located. The top five are:

1. We can't afford the assistive technology (whatever it is).
2. The IT department won't allow us to use it and/or it won't work with our current systems.
3. We can't find a solution that works for all people with disabilities.
4. We've bought it and installed, but no one uses it.
5. Staff can't be expected to remember how to use it or to help users with it.

This wonderful book addresses all of the above obstacles and does so with real-life examples, creative approaches, and pragmatic alternatives.

Jane Vincent is a librarian and has worked for the Center for Accessible Technology (Berkeley, CA) since 1997. She mixes and matches everything from the lowest tech materials to cutting-edge high-tech products to custom fit solutions to specific situations. Her approach is to provide efficiency and comfort for all library users, not just for people with disabilities.

As you read her book, I know that you, too, will be impressed with her extensive knowledge and expertise. Because of her continual reading, her avid curiosity, and her many connections in the assistive technology field, Jane not only knows what is available and possible now, but also what is coming around the corner. As a colleague has said about Jane, "Her vision is sharp, but not narrow; she sees important connections even if they're far afield."

Rhea Joyce Rubin
Library Consultant
http://www.rheajoycerubin.org

Preface

Within the past 20 years, a heartening revolution has started to occur in the perception of people with disabilities. Rather than continuing to be stereotyped as incapable and dependent, disabled people are becoming appreciated as individuals with varied interests and with much to offer the world. Technology, and computer technology in particular, has had an inestimable role in this revolution, facilitating the ability of many people to pursue educational, employment, and personal goals.

However, computer design still assumes uniform capabilities of vision, dexterity, and comprehension among all users. Thus, computers can also create the single largest barrier that people with disabilities still must overcome. This barrier is primarily addressed through use of some of the hundreds of products—commonly known as "assistive technologies"—that modify or replace standard monitors, keyboards, and mice and provide strategies for presenting information in ways that are easier to understand.

You may be aware of people with disabilities who already come to your library and wondered if there were ways to make your computers usable by them. You might have even bought a few products that are advertised for enhancing computer accessibility, such as screen magnifying software or a keyboard labeled as "ergonomic." However, you may still be unclear whether these are providing appropriate accommodations for your patrons.

The purpose of *Implementing Cost-Effective Assistive Computer Technology: A How-To-Do-It Manual for Librarians* is to help library teams make the best possible choices, both initially and on an ongoing basis, about which assistive computer technologies will provide the most appropriate strategies for accommodating patrons with disabilities. It draws extensively on writings about library best practices to ensure that assistive technology implementation is a fully integrated part of your services, not an afterthought.

Reading this book from cover to cover will give you a step-by-step process for getting the maximum payoff from assistive technology implementation for the benefit of people with cognitive, physical, and sensory disabilities, as well as many others who have difficulty using a standard computer. If you're already providing some assistive technology services, the book's organization will let you easily find ideas to strengthen your program.

You'll also find many anecdotes, checklists, templates, and worksheets. The anecdotes are from librarians across the country, most of whom were interviewed specifically for this book. The checklists, templates, and worksheets will help you think about what information you need to gather and what decisions you need to make, and it will give you a practical way to organize your findings so you can take action.

Organization

Implementing Cost-Effective Assistive Computer Technology consists of six chapters, followed by an appendix, glossary, and bibliography.

Assistive technology implementation shouldn't be distinct from your general computer services. By following library best practices starting at the planning process, you will be able to add assistive technology to your current computers with minimal disruption and maximal effectiveness. Chapter 1, "Equal but Not Separate: Integrating Assistive Technology into Your Overall Planning," starts by discussing all patrons—not just those who are clearly covered by the ADA—who would benefit from assistive technology use. It then discusses ways to gather data about appropriate solutions, identify useful community resources, create measurable planning objectives, and set equitable policies. Information about using accessible formats for communication is also included.

Before making informed assistive technology purchase decisions, it's critical to understand why assistive technology is even necessary. The reasons usually involve the inaccessibility of standard equipment, where physical, sensory, or comprehension barriers may exist. Chapter 2, "Understanding Barriers and Solutions," focuses on barriers to use of the standard monitor, keyboard, mouse, computer casing, and workstation and on problems that patrons may have with understanding and creating information content on computers. For each barrier, it presents categories of solutions, with attention given to the relevance of the solution for library environments. These solutions may be available via the computer operating system (both Windows and Macintosh systems are covered), product features, or third-party vendors. It also describes peripherals that may play a role in effective implementation, such as scanners and headphones.

Once you've talked with all interested parties, the next step is to select appropriate categories of solutions from those listed in Chapter 2. Because in many cases there will be more than one way to address barriers, specific products will need to be evaluated for desirability and affordability. Chapter 3, "Selecting the Appropriate Solutions for Your Library," covers how to prioritize acquisition of assistive technology solutions, using established practices for collection development. This includes a look at the benefits and drawbacks of freeware versus commercial products and mainstream versus specialized solutions. It then discusses how to create a justifiable budget for both up-front and hidden costs, including some creative funding strategies, and how to work with product vendors.

Even products that seem ideal for eliminating access barriers still need to be evaluated for compatibility issues. Conflicts can occur because of the existing computer setup, because of the applications or materials being accessed, or even because of issues between two or more assistive technology programs. Chapter 4, "Exploring Compatibility with Other Applications," looks at how to communicate effectively with information technology (IT) staff about potential compatibility issues. It then provides details about the potential causes of these issues: security software, networks, different types of applications, and document formats. To address these issues, it then covers testing for compatibility, communicating with vendors, and addressing situations where technical issues cannot be resolved.

Once assistive technology is in place, the public needs to be informed of its availability and supported in its use. Staff members will need training, not only about the technology, but also about providing appropriate services to its users, including referrals as necessary. Chapter 5, "Communicating with All Relevant Communities," discusses marketing services to potential consumers, including those who may not identify as having disabilities or as computer users. It also provides a guide to training staff members about disability etiquette and assistive technology. Finally, for patrons who require more assistance than the library can provide, it covers working with community resources that provide training, support, and other services.

Like any other technology, assistive hardware and software will occasionally need to be updated. This can be triggered by evaluation results, new product releases, or changes to the library's overall computer setup. Chapter 6, "Keeping Assistive Technology Up-to-Date," covers collecting information on assistive technology use and user demand that can be integrated into the next round of planning. It provides guidance on when and when not to upgrade to new versions of assistive software, as well as potential assistive technology implications when the library's computers are upgraded to a new operating system or otherwise modified. The chapter ends with a look at the future of assistive technology.

The appendix lists several manufacturers of assistive technology products, with annotations indicating each manufacturer's specialty. It also lists several vendors that sell products from multiple manufacturers. Finally, it cites lists of resources for learning about accessibility apps for mobile devices.

The glossary provides short definitions of topics that are mentioned throughout the book. It's intended as an easy way to understand key concepts without having to look for the full definitions elsewhere.

The book ends with a bibliography that provides additional sources of information about many topics related to assistive technology and services to people with disabilities.

To keep this book continually current, there is a companion blog at http://www.janevincent.com/iceact. This resource provides links to and information about new and useful accessibility programs and apps, changes in legislation, innovations in the assistive technology field, and other parallel topics.

Even in the technological age, librarianship remains a service profession, dedicated to ensuring equitable access to information for all. The goal of *Implementing Cost-Effective Assistive Computer Technology* is to provide a guide to all facets of making your computers accessible, not only so your library can meet its legal requirements for equal access, but also so your patrons with disabilities can experience the highest possible level of customer service when using your public computers.

Acknowledgments

This book has multiple root systems. One started in the children's room of the Highland Park (IL) Public Library, where a kindly librarian handed my four-year-old self a primer on elephants and gave me a lifetime appreciation for high, overstuffed bookshelves. Another began at Lawrence University when Ronna Swift introduced me to Larry Minsky, who has shaped my thinking more than even he could ever appreciate. A third came from the Barrier Free Computer Users Group at the University of Michigan, whose spark was started by Doug Thompson and is carried to this day by Jack Bernard.

No author ever had a better fairy godmother than Rhea Rubin, who provided connections, encouragement, access to her personal library, thoughtful insight, and lunch.

Sandy Wood, Charles Harmon, and the staff at Neal-Schuman made the process of writing this book smooth and joyous.

Bay Area Disability Services Librarians (BADSL) is a dedicated group of public librarians and others interested in library accessibility who meet every other month to share wisdom and let me tag along. Particular thanks to Marti Goddard, Lynne Cutler, Alan Bern, and Richard Bray.

Proving that librarians are the soul of generosity, I owe thanks to the many who patiently answered questions, provided stories, and offered support: Donald A. Barclay, Rosemary Griebel, Alan Bern, Heather Robertson, Anna Schnitzer, James Patrick Timony, Richard Tucey, Rhea Rubin, Joan Durrance, Elaine Butler, the Contra Costa County Library Accessibility Committee, Nancy Laskowski, Terry Soave, Paul Signorelli, and Josephine Caron. Others who provided invaluable input were Isanna Palmer, Alan Cantor, Lesley Gibbons, and Peter Mark Roget.

One of the perks of writing a book is having an excuse to spend long hours in handsome libraries. Many thanks to the staff members of the Gardner Library (University of California–Berkeley), the Hatcher and Shapiro Libraries (University of Michigan), and the Berkeley Public Library.

Profound appreciation to my chapter readers: Marti Goddard (Chapter 1), Debra Griffith and Jen McDonald-Peltier (Chapter 2), Betty Lutton and Karen Sheehan (Chapter 3), Isanna Palmer, Alan Bern, and Alan Cantor (Chapter 4), Lynne Cutler and Karen Sheehan (Chapter 5), and Rhea Rubin and Joan Durrance (Chapter 6).

I have been fortunate to interact with many of the best and brightest figures in the assistive technology and disability advocacy fields, including Jim Fruchterman, Danny Chalfen, Alan Brightman, Victor Tsaran, Norm Coombs, Dick Banks, Darola Bray, Nancy Smith, B.A. Scheuers, Cathy Trueba, Bridgett Perry, Lainey Feingold, Ray Grott, Ronny Galt, Marc Sutton, Josh Miele, Neal Ewers, Paul Longmore, Laura Hershey, Roger Smith, Larry Goldberg, Harry Murphy, Russ Holland, Mary Lester, Jackie Brand, Corbett O'Toole, Kathy Martinez, Darlys Van Der Beek, Noel Runyon, and Randy Marsden. Special acknowledgements to Gregg Vanderheiden, pioneer and mentor, and Jim Tobias, who delivers wit and *mitzvot* in equal measure.

Kudos to the Center for Accessible Technology (CforAT): Jen McDonald-Peltier, Karen Sheehan, Jon Mires, Marty Sweeney, Eric Smith, Sally Mirault, and Dmitri Belser, and many former coworkers, particularly Helen Miller, Lisa Wahl, Paul Hendrix, Margaret Cotts, Maggie Morales, Carolyn Byerly-Dean, and Diane Dew.

My gratitude to the extraordinary teachers in my life, especially Vincent Allison, Richard Stowe, Bruce Cronmiller, George Smalley, Dick Yatzeck, Dick Sanerib, Dan Taylor, Joan Durrance, Judy Weedman, and Victor Rosenberg. Marie Lundquist, Kathy Isaacson, Harriet Tippett, and Carol Butts were my early librarian role models.

The disability community in and around Berkeley has been an ongoing source of support and information. Thanks to Culture!Disability!Talent! (Pamela Walker, Liane Yasumoto, Cheryl Marie Wade, Peni Hall, Barbara Duncan, Tony Schmiesing, Noemi Sohn, Afi-Tiombe Kambon, David Roche, Joel Rutledge, David Steinberg, and Michael Horton), Lucy Greco, Karen Marshall, Nina Ghiselli, the members of the Ed Roberts Campus, the Independent Living Resource Center of San Francisco, the residents of Arnieville, and my CforAT clients.

Thanks to my aunts Peggy and Nancy and to my chosen family: Lisa/Sherrie/Bruce and their families, Isa and Connie, Griffy, Julie, Amy, Coyotl, Dr. Jim, Randy, Bang, Schmenkman, Mark, and Deborah. Thank you, Logan. Capradio.org's classical station provided a wonderful soundtrack to write by. A shout-out to Kimberly, Saundra, and the members of my sanity-preserving fiber therapy groups. And a lifetime of skritchies to Madeleine, who put up with occasional late meals and continual distraction and still runs purring up the stairs to meet me every morning.

As this book was being developed, the world suddenly lost a passionate, brilliant, generous, funny, and very dear man. Jim Knox was a quiet titan of assistive technology whose influence was felt at the University of Michigan and well beyond. We grew up in the field side by side, and I relied on his wise insight to find both innovative accommodation strategies and exquisite $1.50 Chinese food. For the many who miss him—especially Roberta, Bill, Linda, Aunt Velma, and their families—it is hoped that the dedication brings some comfort.

Introduction: How to Use This Book

Implementing assistive technology is often perceived as something distinct from a library's other activities, even those that involve computers. It isn't, or at least it shouldn't be. The strategy should address a baseline goal for any library: providing quality products and services that meet identified needs of users.

Therefore, wherever possible, the suggestions in this book are tied to overall library best practices. Several mainstream works on relevant topics are cited in the text and in the Bibliography; consider referring to these for more information about practices that are not yet implemented by your library. Wherever possible, real-life examples of how libraries are using these practices are provided.

However, as with any library function, a one-size-fits-all approach is seldom fruitful. You and your colleagues are the best authorities on your particular library and should modify the suggestions in this book to meet your needs and your established protocols. If you are with a public computer lab in an environment other than a library, also feel free to make modifications as appropriate.

If you have questions or comments, please contact me. My e-mail address is jane@janevincent.com.

Equal but Not Separate:

Integrating Assistive Technology into Your Overall Planning

What Is Assistive Technology?

Computers, especially as a gateway to the Internet, have been an immeasurable boon to people with disabilities. As disability advocate Tom Foley (2010) writes:

> For most people, technology and the Internet provide scales of efficiencies and convenience not dreamt of twenty five years ago. However, for those of us with disabilities, well, old enough to remember, this access represents far more. It represents the first time we have completely independently read and paid bills, followed our favorite team's news, and controlled our banking, investing and retirement planning.

Out of the box, though, computers still aren't usable by many disabled people. Monitor use can be a major problem to anyone who has visual disabilities. The standard keyboard and mouse often present significant barriers. And information may be provided in a way that's hard to access or comprehend.

Over the years, these issues have been addressed by a set of solutions known as "assistive technology." A commonly cited legal definition of assistive technology is, "Any item, piece of equipment, or system, whether acquired commercially, modified, or customized, that is *commonly* [emphasis mine] used to increase, maintain, or improve functional capabilities of individuals with disabilities" (Access Board, 2000). However, sometimes it's the uncommonly used options that are most effective. I find a more useful definition of assistive technology to be simply: "Whatever works."

Assistive technology may be built into the computer's operating system, or incorporated into standard applications such as word processors, or available only from third-party developers. It may be a highly complex piece of electronics, or it may be a strip of Velcro. It may modify existing equipment or may replace it. Assistive technology may be software, hardware, or a combination. It may be free—at least to acquire, if not always to implement—or it may cost thousands of dollars. It may be

The term "assistive technology" is sometimes applied broadly to any product that can be useful to people with disabilities—walkers, grabbers, cutlery with bent handles, portable GPS systems, and so on. This book will focus on assistive technology that facilitates computer use.

The terms "assistive," "adaptive," and "accessible" are used more or less interchangeably in practice when describing technology that can be useful to people with disabilities. For this book, "assistive" is used because it is the term found in legislation such as the Americans with Disabilities Act (ADA) of 1990 and the Assistive Technology Act of 1998. However, performing a web search on any of these terms followed by the word "technology" will likely bring up results of interest.

Assistive technology has a long history of evolving into mainstream products. For example, in Italy around 1808, Pellegrino Turri was eager to invent a way for his blind paramour to write him love letters. His resulting creation is thought to have been the first working typewriter (Taub, 1999).

How does universal design address culture? Ask Jonah Ottensoser, the subject of a *Wired* magazine profile about his job refereeing compatibility between modern kitchen appliances and Orthodox Jewish laws against using machines on the Sabbath (Erard, 2004). Some of the designs he's approved, such as ovens that keep food warm over long time periods, could also be ideal for people with disabilities.

The Census Bureau's definition of "severe" does not necessarily match the level of need for assistive computer technology. For example, all people with learning disabilities are classified by the Census Bureau as having a nonsevere disability, but many of them will need some type of accommodation to understand on-screen information (U.S. Census Bureau, 2005a).

available at your local office supply store, or it may need to be ordered from a single-source vendor.

All assistive technologies do have at least one thing in common: they act as a bridge between existing design and optimal design. They're necessary because computers have been developed to meet a presumed norm of human capability in terms of our dexterity, cognition, and senses. Anyone whose abilities don't meet that norm may find that off-the-shelf technologies aren't going to work well for them. And the further their abilities fall outside the norm, the more difficulty they'll have.

Ideally, assistive technology will eventually be replaced by increased adoption of "universal design," defined as "The design of products and environments to be usable by all people, to the greatest extent possible, without the need for adaptation or specialized design" (Connell et al., 1997). It's a philosophy that encourages development of products and environments that meet the needs of as many people as possible regardless of physical and cognitive ability, language, or culture. Hallmarks of universal design include incorporating multiple strategies for achieving results, providing an intuitive interface, and including fail-safe features. However, until universal design becomes as ubiquitous (read: marketable) as, say, "green" design, libraries and other public computer sites will need to provide assistive technologies so that as many patrons as possible can be accommodated on traditional computers.

Samsung may be the first mainstream company to appreciate the power of universal design as a marketing tool. In 2010, it released a television commercial for its four-door refrigerator that showed a small boy frustrated by being unable to reach light switches, books, or the shelf where his toy dinosaur is sitting but easily able to reach and open a fridge door to retrieve a juice box. Meanwhile, a narrator chirps, "Ever wonder how great it would be if everything was designed with everyone in mind? We did. Introducing the Samsung Four Door Refrigerator..." (Samsung, 2010).

Who Benefits from Assistive Technology?

For linguistic convenience, within much of this book the term "people with disabilities" is going to cast a wide net to include *anyone* for whom a standard computer presents barriers and for whom assistive technology may be appropriate. It can include:

- *People who meet legal or functional definitions of disability.* According to the Census Bureau, in 2005 more than one in five Americans (nearly 50 million people) described themselves as having a disability of some type. Of this population, two out of three describe their disability as severe (U.S. Census Bureau, 2005b).

- *Elders and children.* If you look at product usability studies, most technology is tested with individuals in the 18–24 year age range, who are at the peak of many of their abilities. This leaves out children and elders, who have fluctuating levels of ability. Keep in mind that the number of Americans 65 and older is expected to double between 2010 and 2050 (Vincent and Velkoff, 2010) and that many of these elders will be experienced technology users.

- *People who don't consider themselves disabled.* This may include individuals whose disabilities are caused by repetitive motion—an alarming demographic, especially because these injuries now cause the longest work absences of any type of injury (Bureau of Labor Statistics, 2009: Chart 20). Technology misuse or over-use isn't the sole cause of these injuries, but it's an increasingly more common one.

- *People with temporary disabilities.* This includes not only people recovering from broken wrists or refractive eye surgery but also those who are learning to read or are studying English as a second language.

- *People with beginning computer literacy skills.* These patrons may be working on increasing their skill levels or may need a permanent alternative to the standard computer interface.

When assistive technology is seen as relevant only to a small number of people, it's hard to make a case for its implementation, especially when budgets are tight. Taking the widest possible view of potential users will strengthen your arguments for prioritizing and funding assistive technology.

What Is the Need for Implementing Assistive Technology?

For many libraries, the impetus for installing assistive technology is compliance with the Americans with Disabilities Act (ADA). This is fine as a starting point but shouldn't be the sole, or even primary, focus. The ADA addresses a relatively small subset of the people who actually need to use assistive technology, and many people who are covered by the ADA won't need computer accommodations.

Other incentives may include:

- *Attracting funding sources.* For example, priorities for funding under the Grants to States program of the Library Services and Technology Act (LSTA) include targeting people with disabilities, as well as people from diverse backgrounds, people with low literacy skills, and "persons having difficulty using a library" (Institute of Museum and Library Services, 2011). Chapter 2 contains information about how particular assistive technologies may address the needs of more than one of these groups.

- *Responding to existing user demand.* Frustrated patrons may already be giving you input about computer inaccessibility.

Human capability decreases begin long before eligibility for AARP membership, and there can be creative ways to exploit this. For example, British inventors took advantage of a natural hearing loss in the high-frequency range that starts around age 20 and came up with a loud, high-pitched system that could be blasted to break up groups of local teens congregating in malls without disturbing adults. Instead of complaining, the teens created a ring tone at the same frequency so that they, but not their teachers, could be notified of incoming text messages (Shamah, 2006).

▶ *Companion Blog*

Information about changes to legislation and new resources for relevant grants will be tracked in this book's companion blog at http://www.janevincent.com/iceact.

Consider that for every patron who complains about the difficulty of using standard computers, there are probably several more who either put up with poor design or simply exclude the possibility that they might eventually become computer users.

- *Addressing the library's mission.* Computer access has become a major service provided by libraries, complimentary to rather than competitive with circulation and reference (Daisey, 2010). If your library states that its mission includes providing service to all patrons, ability to take advantage of computer-based services will need to be part of that mission.

The Planning Process

A point that will be reinforced throughout this book is that assistive technology implementation, as much as possible, should not be distinct from the library's existing processes. The techniques discussed here are standard practices for planning new and ongoing initiatives. However, because much of library literature does not take patrons with disabilities into account as part of these practices, additional considerations for addressing this audience are included.

Gathering Data

To ensure that planning will have the maximum positive impact, it is usually necessary to collect data about who your users are and what they need or want. A variety of techniques for gathering data about a target community, including surveys, focus groups, and interviews, are well documented in library literature.

While general data-gathering techniques are as relevant for people with disabilities as for other groups, care needs to be taken to ensure that a holistic approach is in place. A primary key to this approach is ensuring that a variety of communication strategies are in place. This will make other data-gathering projects more meaningful as well because people with disabilities may be a part of any target group. The "Communication Methods and Accessibility Issues" section in this chapter should be referred to as necessary throughout the accessibility implementation process because it is critical to ensure that communication with your target audience is as effective as possible.

Two commonly used methods of gathering data are surveys and focus groups/interviews. Surveys may be distributed in print or electronic formats or delivered through oral interviews via phone or in person. It is vital to be as flexible as possible in allowing people to receive and reply to surveys in the format they prefer. Make sure that questions are clear and concise, and keep them to a minimum because some people may need a significant amount of time to respond to each question. Provide multiple-choice options where possible, but also let people volunteer information that you may not have anticipated.

When you are inviting patrons for group meetings, ask them about what would make them most comfortable. For example, some individuals may prefer to meet with a group that contains only others with their disability type, while others may be fine with a cross-disability group. You should also poll your group members prior to the meeting to help you decide what type of accommodations to provide; for example, if all of your Deaf and hard-of-hearing attendees can follow the conversation via real-time captioning, but only half of them use sign language, then captioning is the clear accommodation choice. If an individual needs an unusual accommodation, or if an individual indicates he or she would feel uncomfortable in a group situation, a one-on-one interview will usually be preferable.

Communication Methods and Accessibility Issues

Standard communication methods, including face-to-face, phone, hard copy materials, materials in electronic format, and audio files, will all be preferred by some people with disabilities and rejected by others. The following is information about each of these methods to keep in mind when conducting focus groups, surveys, and interviews, as well as for day-to-day interactions and for marketing.

Details on specific technology used as part of these solutions are not provided because these may quickly become outdated. Instead, suggestions on finding the latest information are provided in Chapter 3 (pp. 51–52), and specifics on using various methods are provided in the bibliography (p. 132). The Checklist: Tips for Serving People with Disabilities (Chapter 5, pp. 96–97) provides additional information on interacting with people who have specific types of disabilities.

Face-to-Face

Within a group of people who have a common disability, there may be a significant variety of communication methods. Deaf people may use American Sign Language (ASL) or various forms of lipreading; they may also prefer a text-based communication strategy, such as reading a real-time captioning transcript of what is being said. People who are hard of hearing may use hearing aids or portable amplifiers. People with speech disabilities may use devices that produce synthesized speech, may have a human interpreter, or may prefer to use their own voice. As much as possible, these methods should be respected and accommodated. The 2011 amendment to the Title III Americans with Disabilities Act regulations states, "A public accommodation should consult with individuals with disabilities whenever possible to determine what type of auxiliary aid is needed to ensure effective communication, but the ultimate decision as to what measures to take rests with the public accommodation, provided that the method chosen results in effective communication" (U.S. Department of Justice, 2010: 56253).

You may also need to modify your standard communication strategies for people with cognitive or emotional disabilities. For example, some people may find eye contact intimidating and may signal this either by

> Deafness is seen by many individuals as a cultural and linguistic distinction, not a medical condition or a disability. It has become customary to capitalize the word "Deaf" when it refers to Deaf culture or its members, as opposed to using "deaf" to indicate the inability to hear.

informing you or by avoiding your gaze. Take your cue from them and respond accordingly.

Telephone

Although the telephone was in part the result of Alexander Graham Bell's experiments in creating "visible speech" devices for his Deaf students, it caused a huge barrier for both Deaf people and people with speech disabilities during most of the twentieth century (Gorman, 2005). A breakthrough solution, circa 1964, was the teletypewriter (TTY; sometimes known as a "telecommunication device for the Deaf," TDD, or "text telephone"). Because TTY use requires that analogous equipment be available at both ends of the call, some libraries have installed TTY equipment to communicate with patrons who can't use a standard telephone.

At the beginning of the twenty-first century, TTY use has been largely abandoned in favor of mainstream text-based communication: texting and instant messaging for real-time communication and e-mail for other purposes. Some digital cell phones have a mode that lets them communicate directly with a TTY. Smartphone apps may also play a role; for example, ProLoquo2Go is an app that lets users who can't speak or type communicate over an iPhone by selecting pictures that have corresponding auditory output. If you don't already have a TTY, don't put one in. Instead, look at ways your library might take advantage of text messaging, e-mail, and other mainstream communication options to interact with Deaf individuals and people with speech disabilities.

Individuals who are still using a TTY, or who have access only to a standard phone, can take advantage of the nationwide Telecommunications Relay Service (TRS), which allows anyone to dial 711 and initiate a phone call using an intermediary operator at no charge. These operators have access to TTYs; they are also trained to act as interpreters for people with difficult-to-understand speech.

As part of your staff training (see Chapter 5), make sure that staff members understand how to make and receive 711 calls; instructions are available at http://www.fcc.gov/cgb/consumerfacts/711.html. Make sure that staff members initially assume that silence or difficult-to-understand speech on the other end of the phone indicates a call from someone with a disability. Encourage them to make a reasonable effort to engage the caller.

Video phones have had a rocky history and have yet to find mainstream acceptance. People who speak ASL, however, have embraced them as a natural strategy for communicating with other ASL speakers. Some libraries have installed video phones onsite; the equipment (but not the connection) may be furnished at no charge by the manufacturer. The video phones at the Oakland and San Francisco public libraries, among others, have proved quite popular among Deaf patrons.

Print

For most people with low vision, large print will be useful. The primary exception will be people with glaucoma or other causes of peripheral vision loss; these patrons will likely prefer standard size print. Some people with learning or cognitive disabilities may prefer large print.

The generally recommended font specifications are 16 or 18 point sans-serif typeface, such as Arial. The American Printing House for the Blind (APH) makes the APHont font, based on its research about legibility, available for free to benefit people with low vision. The registration form required for downloading the font is available at http://www.aph .org/products/aphont_get.html.

Contrast between text and background colors is also an important consideration. Black text on a white background causes glare and legibility problems for many people with visual or learning disabilities. A light gray or pastel background is preferable.

Braille

Braille is used by only a small percentage of blind people, usually those who are congenitally blind and learned it as children. Statistics show that only about 12 percent of blind children currently read braille, even though braille literacy appears to be a significant factor in employment (Braille Institute of America, 2011). People who become blind later in life tend not to learn braille, often because they believe that audio-based solutions, such as screen readers and Talking Books, have a shorter learning curve. Another reason may be because their blindness is a secondary effect of illnesses such as diabetes or AIDS, which can also cause fingertip neuropathy and make braille letters difficult to read.

In-house braille production requires use of software that converts standard text to a braille format and a braille printer. Braille printers generally cost $2,000 and up and can be very noisy. Unless you are going to be producing a large amount of braille materials or are providing braille printer access to your patrons, you may find it more cost effective to contract out braille production. A nationwide list of braille transcription resources is at http://www.nfb.org/nfb/Braille_transcription.asp.

Braille comes in multiple "flavors." The most common are Grade 1, which provides letter-for-letter transcription, and Grade 2, which uses some shortcuts ("contractions") for common words such as "children," which is contracted to two braille letters, and frequent letter combinations such as "ing," which is contracted to a single letter. Find out from your focus groups which grade they would prefer for receiving materials.

Websites and E-mail

A summary of reasons why users with disabilities may not be able to use specific websites are covered briefly in Chapter 4 (pp. 71–72), but in practice web accessibility is a massive topic. Instead of trying to cover it in the scope of this book, information about seminal resources is listed in the bibliography (p. 131).

Free e-mail accounts are available through Yahoo!, Google (Gmail), and a variety of other resources. Consider providing a list with several options to patrons who do not already have an e-mail account, and amend the list as necessary to incorporate feedback about which services do or do not work well with particular assistive technologies.

Accessibility camps are emerging as a way for individuals to get together and share information about accessibility of websites and other electronic media. Presenters are not scheduled ahead of time; instead, attendees are asked to come prepared to speak on a variety of topics. Information on past and upcoming accessibility camps is at http://www.accessibilitycamp.org/; a "how-to" on sponsoring an accessibility camp is at http://www.accessibilitycamp.org/howto.shtml.

Keep in mind that if patrons with disabilities are accessing the Internet only at the library, a web-based means of disseminating or gathering information will probably not be sufficient as a sole communication method. In particular, these patrons may be reluctant to spend any of their limited time on the computer filling out surveys. Redundant formats should always be available.

Electronic and Audio Formats

Even if they don't have access to computers outside the library, your patrons may have other devices such as MP3 players and smartphones that can access downloaded audio, video, or text files. Talk to your focus groups about their preferred formats for receiving information. If you have printed materials that need to be accessed by people who need audio formats, take advantage of assistive technologies that convert text to audio files (see Chapter 2, p. 40).

There are a wide variety of electronic text formats available, not all of which provide equal levels of accessibility. PDF is particularly notorious for causing problems; if it's used, make sure another format is available as well.

Establishing Strategic Partnerships

Most communities will already have some organizations that address the needs of people with disabilities either in general or specific to computer use. These organizations may have significant roles to play in helping with your assistive technology program:

- *Recruitment.* Community partners can identify their existing patrons who may be good candidates for participating in your focus groups or interviews. They can also distribute your surveys or notify patrons about them. Once your services are in place, partners can notify patrons and possibly help steer them in the library's direction. For example, if a retirement community has its own buses, it might schedule regular trips to the library.

- *Input.* Staff at partner organizations may be able to discuss best practices that they've developed or trends among their patrons' requests. They may be individuals with disabilities themselves, in which case their input will be even more valuable.

- *Continuity.* Partners may be able to help identify service gaps within your community. Working together to address these will help you both increase your levels of service. For example, there may be time slots when the library computer lab is open but none of the partners' labs are. The partners can then advertise your new accessible computers to their patrons who have requested additional hours for computer use.

- *Information sharing.* Partners who have already implemented assistive computer technology may be able to share information about their experiences. You may also be able to share information about topics such as funding resources or working with local government.

- *Resource sharing.* Working together may permit accomplishment of goals that would not be possible independently. For example, if the library and another agency both see the need for a relatively expensive or large piece of equipment, neither may be able to acquire it independently. However, you may decide that you are able to split the cost or that the agency could fund the equipment while the library houses it.

Places to contact about developing partnerships can include:

- *Existing library resources.* Make sure the people responsible for any literacy groups are involved in your planning process. Individuals who volunteer with the library—for example, legal aid consultants—may be interacting with individuals with disabilities and may have insight to provide. If you have already identified patrons with disabilities who are requesting accommodations, you will want to ask for their input about agencies to contact.

- *Disability organizations (for-profit or nonprofit).* Start with any agencies listed under "Disability Services" in your local Yellow Pages. Try doing an Internet search for "disability" or specific disability types in your city or county (e.g., "Cerebral Palsy" "East Helena"). Look in the government section of your phone book for your local Department of Rehabilitation office (often listed under "Rehabilitation"); they are tasked with helping people with disabilities find employment. Also try doing a search for charitable initiatives that address a particular type of disability; for example, both Lions Clubs and Delta Gamma sororities focus on services to people with visual disabilities.

- *Educational institutions.* Check with the special education department in your local school district and the Disabled Student Services office at any nearby colleges and universities. Some postsecondary institutions may have assistive technology labs; for example, all California community colleges are mandated to have a High-Tech Center that provides demonstrations and training for their students with disabilities.

- *Elder-focused resources.* Many senior centers and retirement communities now have computer labs and instructors. They may also have attendees/residents who would be interested in providing input to the library.

- *Government resources.* Your municipal government may have a commission on disability. It may also be worth looking for local legislators who have demonstrated an interest in addressing the needs of people with disabilities in your community or in general.

- *Hospitals and other medical resources.* Local medical professionals may be able to pass information about your accessible computer lab to their patients. Hospitals may have support groups for

---

PLANNING IN ACTION

Pueblo County–City (CO) Library District

The Pueblo County–City Library District (PCCLD) in Colorado began a formal process of implementing assistive computer technology in 2004. In addition to surveying patrons and community resources, it convened a 16-member Advisory Board, designed to "represent a broad coalition of persons who use assistive technology or whose organizations provide services to persons in Pueblo County" (Tucey, 2007). An article in the 2007 *Colorado Libraries* special issue on libraries and accessibility describes how this board became invaluable to the implementation process:

> At the initial meeting of the Advisory Board with PCCLD's Assistive Technology Committee in June 2007, board members were asked to respond to the following three questions in order to obtain their input and support for PCCLD's plan for implementing assistive technology in 2007 and 2008:
>
> 1. What things are we (PCCLD) already doing well for our customers with disabilities?
> 2. What are the functional needs of the disabled when they visit the Library?
> 3. What are the three most important things that the Library should consider doing to improve access for our customers?
>
> The Advisory Board's responses to these three questions were especially helpful. Using the responses, the Library District developed its assistive technology project and submitted an application for funding in July and August 2007 to the Friends of the Pueblo City–County Library District (a $1,250 request), and to the Colorado State Library (a $20,000 LSTA project request). With $21,250 in total funding now received from these sources the project began as planned with a subsequent Advisory Board meeting in October 2007. (Tucey, 2007)

(*Source*: Reprinted with permission from Pueblo City–County Library District [PCCLD].)

---

people with disabilities. Attendant care organizations can help reach people who might not easily be able to visit the library.

Creating a Plan

Several books are available about best practices libraries should use in planning. The suggestions in this chapter are based on the approach outlined by Sandra Nelson (2008) in *Strategic Planning for Results*. However, if your library uses a different approach, feel free to modify these suggestions as appropriate.

Nelson recommends defining objectives through use of four measures: people served, how well the service meets the needs of people served, total units of service provided, and outcome measurement (Nelson, 2008: 96). All of these are relevant to objectives around implementing assistive technology:

- *People served*. Consider all of the categories listed under "Who Benefits from Assistive Technology?" earlier in this chapter. Statistics about people with disabilities, children, and elders can be gleaned from census data. Other information can be gathered from in-house data about prior service to target patrons, such as attendance at literacy programs. Based on this information, set goals for both the total number of individuals served and the total number of visits. For example, if you estimate the target audience in your community is approximately 2,500 people, you might decide that within three years, at least 400 of them will have used your adapted computers (total individuals served = 400) and that each of them will use the computers an average of four times (total number of visits = 400 × 4 = 1,600). If you plan to provide trainings, programs, or other services to people with disabilities, include goals for these as well.

- *How well the service meets the needs of the people served.* This covers user feedback about your services. For example, goals might include, "80 percent of patrons with disabilities surveyed report that their needs are accommodated by the current assistive technology setup."

- *Total units of service provided.* This measures service transactions. You may decide that this is covered by "people served," or you may decide to measure usage of specific assistive technologies, for example, "Trackballs and other alternative mice will be checked out from the circulation desk 500 times."

- *Outcome measurement.* While "how well the service meets the needs . . ." addresses user satisfaction with your program, outcome measurement addresses the program's impact. You will be looking for information about how use of accessible computers and related library services has impacted the lives of members of your target audience.

Joan Durrance and Karen Fisher have outlined several common, measurable types of outcomes for any user feedback process: attitude changes, increased ability to access information, confidence building, skill development, knowledge gains, social networking, and status changes. They suggest an if–then thought process for identifying outcomes (Durrance and Fisher, 2005). When applied to people with disabilities, this process might include "*If* we want to promote educational and employment opportunities for people with disabilities (status change), *then* we need to provide accessible ways for them to interact with websites," or "*If* we want people with disabilities to communicate with far-off friends and family (social networking), *then* we need to help them set up and use a free Facebook account." Because so many facets of modern life revolve around the ability to use e-mail, the Internet, and standard applications, it should be reasonably easy to use if–then strategies to identify relevant outcomes.

The next step is to develop measurable goals based on these outcomes. For example, goals based on the above if–then statements might include "25 percent (50) of people who used our adapted computers will report that they applied for a job online" or "70 percent of the people who attended our e-mail training report that they came back to the library and used e-mail at least twice."

Developing Priority Usage Policies

The only time users should receive unequal treatment is when it is called for in library policies. . . . Of course some might argue that providing extra assistance to users with disabilities is unequal treatment, but the counter argument is that the extras provided to users with disabilities are intended only to level the playing field with non-disabled users. After all, the Americans with Disabilities Act calls for "reasonable accommodations," not "unfair advantage." (Barclay, 2000: 207)

Human ability occurs on a continuum. For example, less than 1 percent of the U.S. population meets the legal definition of blindness (National Eye Institute, 2010). At the other end of the continuum are people with better than 20/20 vision. The majority of us fall in between these extremes. We may already use certain personalized assistive technologies, otherwise known as glasses or contact lenses, to augment our vision. However, some people on the continuum won't benefit from corrective eyewear or don't find it lets them effectively access a computer screen.

Assistive technology is on a continuum as well: a continuum of desirability. Most blind people access computers via screen-reader software, which provides a holistic auditory substitute for looking at the monitor. But almost no one who doesn't have to use a screen reader is going to want to use one. For one thing, by default screen readers speak a great deal of information about the status of a page, such as the number of links on a website. This information is useful to a blind person but will be annoying to most sighted people. Simpler speech output programs, however, may find a level of demand not only among people with learning or cognitive disabilities but also among people with standard vision whose eyes are tired or who want to use auditory output as a proofreading aid. And many people, regardless of their visual acuity, will opt for computers with large-screen monitors if available.

To ensure that people who must use assistive technology can get access to the computers where it is installed, some type of policies need to be in place. These should cover the range of accommodations that the library is willing to provide for computer users with disabilities, including, but not necessarily limited to, use of assistive technologies, and the appropriate strategies for giving one patron priority over another.

Your library may already have established general policies related to computer use, including Internet use (such as covering whether the library uses a filter to limit or prohibit access to questionable websites) and public computer use (such as the level of assistance that staff members are expected to provide). You may wish to start by examining these policies and deciding which, if any, need to be modified to address the needs of people with disabilities. If your library does not have general policies in place, or if they do not seem relevant for covering the needs of people with disabilities, the Accommodation Policy Template on page 13 is intended as a starting place.

One of the most popular computer accommodations that many libraries provide is extended time—allowing patrons with disabilities to reserve computers for, say, two hours when most patrons can get only a one-hour reservation. This can qualify as accommodation for a variety of reasons, including the following:

- Many of the assistive technology programs discussed in Chapter 2 allow users to choose their own settings. Because security

Look at the relevance of modifying other policies as well. For example, the San Francisco Public Library's "Guidelines for Library Use" includes the statement, "Library users who wish to request a reasonable modification of these guidelines because of a disability or health problem may contact library staff or may call the Library's Access Services Manager." (San Francisco Public Library, 2007)

Accommodation Policy Template

Policy Questions to Address

1. Does the library provide assistive computer technology? Which computers is it provided on?
2. How does providing assistive technology support the library's goals and objectives?

Definitions

1. What does the library mean by "person with a disability"?
2. What does the library mean by "assistive technology"?

Regulation Questions to Address

1. Does the library require people with a disability to self-identify before they can request and receive accommodations? If so, how is this handled? Do they have to go through a registration process with the library?
2. May any library customer use computers that have assistive technology software installed? If not, who may use them?
3. May any library customer use assistive technology hardware that is permanently installed (e.g., large print monitors)? If not, who may use them?
4. May any library customer use assistive technology hardware that can be checked out and used with any library computer (e.g., alternative mice, scanners)? If not, who may use them?
5. Will the amount and type of assistance that library staff provides to people with disabilities be different from that provided to the general public? If so, how will it differ?
6. Will exceptions to standard computer security practices be made (e.g., providing access to control panels so that patrons can use accessibility settings)? How and under what conditions will this be done?
7. Will the library permit people with disabilities to bring and use their own assistive hardware? If so, are there any restrictions on this (e.g., hardware must have a USB connector)?
8. Will the library permit people with disabilities to bring and use their own assistive technology software on a flash drive or other portable media? If so, are there any restrictions on this (e.g., the media must be scanned for viruses before being used on a public computer)?
9. Will the library prioritize use of assistive technology by people with disabilities over nondisabled persons? If so, how will this be enforced?
10. Will the library prioritize use of assistive technology by some people with disabilities over others (e.g., people with learning disabilities over people in the library literacy program)? If so, how will this be enforced?
11. If a person covered by the priority use regulations is eligible to use a computer that is currently used by a nondisabled person or a person with lower priority, how will the library handle moving the person already at the computer? If this person refuses to move, how will this be handled?
12. Will the library grant extra computer time to patrons with disabilities? If so, how will it be determined who is eligible for this accommodation?
13. Will other existing library policies be modified to address the needs of people with disabilities? Which ones, and how will they be modified?

(*Source*: Based on the templates in Nelson, Sandra, and June Garcia. 2003. *Creating Policies for Results: From Chaos to Clarity*. Chicago: American Library Association.)

software is unlikely to permit individuals' settings to be maintained between sessions (see Chapter 4), patrons will need extra time to implement their preferences before carrying out their Internet or application use. Many libraries consider it fair to provide this time.

Implementing Cost-Effective Assistive Computer Technology

POLICY MAKING IN ACTION

Berkeley (CA) Public Library

Berkeley was the birthplace of the first Independent Living Center and is often thought to be the first city to provide sidewalk curbcuts, so it's not surprising that the Berkeley Public Library (BPL) has put a lot of thought into accommodating patrons with disabilities.

Alan Bern, BPL Special Services Coordinator, shares his experiences with establishing policies around computer use.

Upon my arrival at Berkeley Public Library (BPL) in 1997, part of my job as Special Services Coordinator was to work with disabled patrons to provide appropriate services as well as accommodations when requested. At that time BPL had an accommodation for disabled patrons to double their check out time period on books. This extension did NOT apply to other library materials at that time, nor was there a request for such.

We trusted patrons to let us know if they were disabled and that they needed this extension. Obviously, not all disabled patrons needed, nor asked for, the extension. Some who requested the extension were probably not, by the letter of the law, disabled. Our motto at that time: *If someone spends a lot of their time "proving" that they are disabled, it's best (and easiest) to take their word for it.*

I believe that checkouts were increased manually by staff at that time, but our software vendor allowed us to create patron types which made this increased checkout automatic and "invisible," a good thing in terms of seamless accommodation.

In 1999 BPL began to formalize the process by having patrons sign up with an application. The original impetus grew out of a need to formalize and regularize the process: it was not so much anything exactly legal, but we wanted to be fair and consistent and offer accommodations as appropriate in a balanced fashion. It was a way, also, for staff to all be on the same page: for example, we did not want individual staff members "deciding" whether someone needed extra checkout time. Fortunately there was BADSL [Bay Area Disability Services Librarians, a local consortium of librarians charged with implementing accessibility], and we learned from each other. In this case I modeled our registration process directly off Lynne Cutler's at Oakland Public Library.

In 2003, Proxies were formally added to the application process to allow people to designate someone to pick up and return items. This was especially important to those patrons living outside of Berkeley because they do not qualify for our Outreach to the Homebound library services. We do not require proof of the "inability to get to the library" for these patrons.

Also in 2003, proof of disability became a requirement to get an Extended Services library card. The reason that we found it necessary to require proof of disability was the stated need for increased computer time by many disabled patrons. This increased time period was worked out with City of Berkeley Disability Specialist Paul Church as a legal and fair accommodation. Since, in fact, all of our computer users need/want increased time, but there is scarcity based on our budget, limited IT staff time, and limited physical space for computers, we needed to limit use of these computers. Because the reservation software we use (and all reservation software packages we know) do NOT let one reserve based on the patron type, but rather only by computer type matched to patron type, we decided to limit users of our accessible computers to those with proof of disability. Initially we would get complaints from patrons that the accessible computers were not being used so why couldn't they use them—now they are occupied most of the time by disabled users so this is hardly an issue. Having 975 Extended Services patrons is the difference since many of these users want increased computer time.

(*Source:* Alan Bern, e-mail communication, October 27, 2010, and November 22, 2010.)

- If assistive technology is used, extra time will generally be needed to perform most tasks. For example, reviewing a webpage by listening to it via screen-reader software is much slower than viewing it. Screen readers don't have sophisticated ways to mimic the visual capability of glancing randomly around a page and focusing on the most pertinent information. It can therefore be considered fair to allow screen-reader users more time to use the computer.

- Even if persons with a disability do not need to use the assistive technology, it may be onerous for them to travel to the library on a regular basis due to factors such as limited availability of paratransit (buses that transport people with disabilities via nonfixed routes on an on-call basis). It may therefore be fair to give them more time when they do get to your library.

Naturally, if you provide extra computer time and word gets out, your percentage of patrons with "disabilities" may rise exponentially. You will need to create a specific policy about how patrons can request and be granted this accommodation.

Summary

Providing assistive technology is a process. It can be rather like a chess game: if you can see several steps ahead, you'll be more prepared to meet the idiosyncrasies that will occur along the way. The more you can prepare—by identifying all potentially interested parties, by getting their buy-in and participation, by knowing how to provide a variety of communication strategies, and by developing usage policies—the better informed your process of selecting solutions will be. You can then go on to review the range of potential solutions, which are presented in Chapter 2.

▶ **Companion Blog**
For resource updates, visit this book's companion blog at http://www.janevincent.com/iceact.

References

Access Board. 2000. "Electronic and Information Technology Accessibility Standards." United States Access Board. http://www.access-board.gov/sec508/standards.htm.

Barclay, Donald A. 2000. *Managing Public-Access Computers*. New York: Neal-Schuman.

Braille Institute of America. 2011. "Facts about Sight Loss and Definitions of Blindness." Braille Institute. Accessed February 21. http://www.brailleinstitute.org/facts_about_sight_loss.

Bureau of Labor Statistics. 2009. "2008 Nonfatal Occupational Injuries and Illnesses, Private Industry." U.S. Bureau of Labor Statistics. http://www.bls.gov/iif/oshwc/osh/case/osch0040.pdf.

Connell, Bettye Rose, Mike Jones, Ron Mace, Jim Mueller, Abir Mullick, Elaine Ostroff, et al. 1997. "The Principles of Universal Design." The Center for Universal Design, North Carolina State University. http://www.ncsu.edu/www/ncsu/design/sod5/cud/about_ud/udprinciples text.htm.

Daisey, Jaime. 2010. "Computer Access and Traditional Library Services." *Fast Facts*. Library Research Service. http://www.lrs.org/documents/fastfacts/283_Computers_and_Libraries.pdf.

Durrance, Joan, and Karen Fisher. 2005. *How Libraries and Librarians Help*. Chicago: American Library Association.

Erard, Michael. 2004. "The Geek Guide to Kosher Machines." *Wired* 12, no. 11: 166–169.

Foley, Tom. 2010. "For People with Disabilities, Technology Is Disproportionately Empowering!" *The Podium* (blog), August 17. http://internetinnovation .org/blog/comments/for-people-with-disabilities-technology-is-dispropor tionatcly-empowering.

Gorman, Mike. 2005. "Alexander Graham Bell's Path to the Telephone." University of Virginia. Last modified June 24. http://www2.iath.virginia .edu/albell/.

Institute of Museum and Library Services. 2011. "Grants to State Library Administrative Agencies." Institute of Museum and Library Services. Accessed February 21. http://www.imls.gov/programs/programs.shtm.

National Eye Institute. 2010. "Statistics and Data: Prevalence of Blindness Data." National Eye Institute. Last modified in August. http://www.nei .nih.gov/eyedata/pbd_tables.asp.

Nelson, Sandra S. 2008. *Strategic Planning for Results*. Chicago: American Library Association.

Nelson, Sandra, and June Garcia. 2003. *Creating Policies for Results: From Chaos to Clarity*. Chicago: American Library Association.

Samsung. 2010. "Refrigerator Wonder." Television commercial. Samsung. http://www.youtube.com/watch?v=ELEPDtLA2CE.

San Francisco Public Library. 2007. "Guidelines for Library Use." San Francisco Public Library. Last modified August 16. http://sfpl.org/index.php?pg= 2000004201.

Shamah, David. 2006. "Digital World: Getting the Buzz." *Jerusalem Post*, June 20. www.jpost.com/Home/Article.aspx?id=25414.

Taub, Eric A. 1999. "The Blind Leading the Sighted." *New York Times*, October 28. http://www.nytimes.com/1999/10/28/technology/the-blind-leading-the-sighted.html.

Tucey, Richard. 2007. "Accessible Avenues: Paving the Way for Patrons with Special Needs." *Colorado Libraries* 33, no. 4: 20–24.

U.S. Census Bureau. 2005a. "Definition of Disability, Functional Limitations, Activities of Daily Living (ADLs), and Instrumental Activities of Daily Living (IADLs)." U.S. Census Bureau. http://www.census.gov/hhes/www/ disability/sipp/disab02/ds02f1.pdf.

———. 2005b. "Prevalence of Disability among Individuals 15 Years and Older by Specific Measures of Disability: 2005." U.S. Census Bureau. http:// www.census.gov/hhes/www/disability/sipp/disab05/d05tb1.pdf.

U.S. Department of Justice. 2010. "Nondiscrimination on the Basis of Disability by Public Accommodations and in Commercial Facilities." *Federal Register* 75, no. 178: 56236-58. http://edocket.access.gpo.gov/2010/2010- 21824.htm.

Vincent, Grayson K., and Victoria A. Velkoff. 2010. "The Next Four Decades: The Older Population in the United States: 2010 to 2050." U.S. Census Bureau. http://www.aoa.gov/aoaroot/aging_statistics/future_growth/ DOCS/p25-1138.pdf.

Understanding Barriers and Solutions

There are many definitions of "disability"—legal, functional, and so on. The one that may be most useful is sometimes referred to as the "environmental" definition: "Disability can be defined as a lack of fit between a person's goals, his or her capabilities, and the resources in the environment" (Meng, 1990: 181). What's powerful about this definition is that it permits flexibility both in identifying who is disabled within in a given environment and in how their "lack of fit"—which can also be called a "barrier"—is addressed.

For a small example of how this goals/capabilities/resources definition works, let's say you're at a conference with a blind colleague. An important contact hands both of you her business card, asks you to call her in a half hour, and walks off. You start to read the card, only to realize it's entirely in braille. Your colleague, who is fluent in braille, reads and pockets the card; no barriers experienced. You, on the other hand, are faced with a rather large barrier. It's possible, but unlikely, for you to change your capabilities by running off and learning enough about braille in a half hour to read the card. You are also unlikely to change your goal of calling the contact because she is well-known for providing generous funding to libraries. The barrier will probably be addressed only if you can find an environmental resource, such as a person who can read the card to you—your colleague, perhaps.

Librarians aren't social workers or career counselors, so we don't usually work to change people's goals. We're not doctors, teachers, or physical therapists, so we don't address people's capabilities. That leaves modifying environmental resources, in this case by adding assistive technology to computer workstations. This can be both the easiest and trickiest way to eliminate barriers. Easy, because there are so many options available that there is some way to accommodate nearly anyone. Tricky, because there are so many options available that it's not always clear which will be most cost-effective for accommodating the largest possible number of patrons in public settings.

This chapter is an introduction to various types of assistive computer technology so that you can interpret results from your focus groups and interviews and become aware of other options that might be relevant. In

Chapters 3 and 4, we'll look at winnowing your options so that you're selecting the solutions that are most appropriate for your patrons, your budget, and your computing environment.

Chapter Organization

Major assistive technology manufacturers and vendors are listed in the appendix (pp. 119–122). A wide range of existing resources provide up-to-date information about assistive technology, the best of which are listed in the "Identifying Options" section of Chapter 3. Some of these are organized by disability type, which may not be useful to public computer labs planning accommodations for a wide variety of people rather than a single individual. This organization strategy also does not address the needs of people who cannot use a standard computer for reasons other than the traditional definitions of disability.

Other resources are organized by type of assistive technology. This is useful if you already know something about the jargon associated with the solutions you are looking for but less so if you are exploring assistive technology for the first time.

This chapter is instead organized by the six areas of computer interaction where individuals are most likely to encounter access barriers:

- Monitor
- Keyboard
- Mouse
- Comprehension
- Computer casing
- Workstation (furniture, lighting)

For the first four areas, the following topics are discussed:

- *Issues and key strategies.* Who is likely to have difficulty with this area? What sort of difficulties might they experience? This topic is designed to encourage thinking about the breadth of patrons who might be running into barriers whether or not they are communicating these to staff. It also summarizes the most common strategies for addressing these barriers.

- *Operating system solutions.* Most operating systems have many built-in accessibility tools. This topic provides an overview of what's available in Windows XP and higher and in the higher versions of Macintosh OS X. Because the names of the tools tend to stay consistent but the path for finding them may change, minimal specific information is given. However, it's easy to search for documentation online using the names of the tools and the relevant operating system for the most accurate setup information. Note that the library's security software may prevent access to some or all of these tools; ways to address this are discussed in Chapter 4.

Microsoft and Apple both maintain comprehensive websites dedicated to information about their built-in accessibility features. These are at http://www.microsoft.com/enable/ and http://www.apple.com/accessibility/.

A few libraries use the Linux operating system on their public access computers. Linux has most of the built-in features discussed here. However, relatively few third-party options are available for this platform.

- *Solutions within popular applications.* Some applications—especially programs that are part of the Microsoft Office suite and popular browsers—have access solutions built in. This topic covers solutions designed with accessibility in mind, as well as some that are less obvious but have proven useful. These are the types of solutions least likely to cause problems, because they do not depend on interaction between multiple applications. Because implementation of these solutions may change significantly between product releases, you will find the most accurate information if you check your current product's "Help" documentation. Keywords to try include "accessibility," "disabilities," or adjectives related to what you want the solution to accomplish (e.g., to find information about increasing text size, "larger" will generally bring up better results than "magnification" or "vision"). If that doesn't work, try looking online for documentation from other resources.

- *Third-party solutions.* This covers all categories of products that are not part of standard computers or applications—software and hardware, free and not, available online or through other means. In a few cases, third-party products are listed under more than one barrier area; their appropriateness is discussed relevant to each barrier.

- *Creative solutions.* Sometimes the best solutions come from unusual sources, such as craft and hardware stores. This topic covers offbeat but effective strategies that are generally inexpensive and easy to implement.

- *Checklists.* These summarize important considerations for third-party products. The checklists are intended to be used as part of the product selection process.

Types of Products Covered

This chapter covers the most relevant types of assistive technology as of this writing, including many that libraries and other public computer labs have implemented, but it is not exhaustive. You may hear about other technologies as a result of focus groups or interviews, through news sources, or elsewhere. The selection processes outlined in Chapters 3 and 4 should be relevant regardless of the product type.

Some of these products would not be cost-effective for most public computing environments, usually because they are prohibitively expensive or need to be highly customized to a single user. However, because people may ask about any and all products without being aware of their cost or complexity, information about a broad range of options is included to help you respond to inquiries. Depending on your situation, even expensive or complex solutions may still be appropriate—for example, you may determine that a significant number of your patrons are experienced and enthusiastic users of refreshable braille technology,

▶ **Companion Blog**

Information about new and notable assistive technology products, including changes in new operating systems, will be tracked in this book's companion blog at http://www.janevincent.com/iceact.

and you have a local branch of the Lions Clubs (one of several charitable organizations for whom blind access is a priority) willing to fund the purchase of an appropriate device.

As with any type of commercial product, assistive technologies go in and out of availability. Sometimes this means the discontinuation of a specific product; sometimes it means that an entire product category has become outdated. Rather than date this book by using specific information, this chapter covers product categories, while the "Identifying Options" section of Chapter 3 covers resources for researching currently available options. In a few cases where there is a unique or exceptional product available, it is discussed by name.

Monitor Barriers

The basic design of most technologies assumes some ability to see, which is an obvious barrier to blind individuals. It can also affect people with various types of permanent or temporary visual impairments, including age-related vision changes, conditions such as macular degeneration, cataracts, and glaucoma, colorblindness, or recuperation from surgery. A great deal of development effort has gone into solutions that either modify or provide an alternative to the visual presentation of information.

Issues and Key Strategies

Reasons that individuals might experience monitor barriers include the following:

- Issue: Inability to see the screen
  - Strategy: Provide an alternative means of accessing output, through audio and/or refreshable braille.
- Issue: Difficulty seeing all onscreen materials

  Issue: Difficulty seeing specific materials (particularly websites) because of their poor design: small print, insufficient text/background color contrast, and so forth
  - Strategy: Make onscreen materials easier to see. This usually involves increasing or decreasing the size of text and icons, changing the typeface, modifying color contrast, or providing redundant speech output.

Some individuals are able to see the screen but can't interpret some or all information. Their accommodations, many of which overlap in function with the accommodations in this section, are covered under Comprehension Barriers (pp. 37–42).

Operating System Solutions

- *Appearance settings.* Windows has long had a variety of built-in options for changing text size and color contrast. Unfortunately, as product development has moved from Windows XP to Vista to Windows 7, these options have become increasingly less useful. For example, in XP about three dozen preset "skins" are available. Choosing a skin changes the system's default font, font size, font color, and background color—for example, "High Contrast Black" provides white text on a black background, and "Windows Standard (Extra Large)" uses standard colors but larger fonts. In Vista, this was cut down to eight skins, none of which use large print. It is possible to set custom preferences, but this involves significant effort, because all elements (dialogue boxes, window titles, icon labels, etc.) need to be adjusted separately. In Windows 7, there are only six high-contrast skins, and none of these uses large print.

Macintosh OS X has a few options for changing color contrast. These include inverting black-on-white system text to white-on-black and using a Grayscale mode that puts a virtual gray filter on the screen.

- *Magnification utilities.* Releases from Windows XP on include a Magnifier utility, which unlike the Display settings has increased in quality in new versions. Windows 7 has a fairly sophisticated Magnifier with a much cleaner interface than prior versions.

  Macintosh systems have a Zoom feature that provides up to 20× magnification. However, letters appear increasingly more distorted the higher the magnification level is set so that they will still be difficult to read for many people.

- *Speech output.* Narrator is a small speech output utility in Windows that provides some access for blind users. As free third-party screen readers become more robust (see "Third Party Solutions," later), the need for reliance on Narrator as an access solution will be minimal. However, it may still be useful in some situations. For example, if third-party screen readers are unable to read a sign-in screen, it's worth checking whether Narrator will work instead.

  Macintosh operating systems 10.4 (Tiger) and newer include a full-featured screen reader called VoiceOver. VoiceOver is also provided in other Apple products such as the iPhone and iPad.

- *Pointer options.* For some people with low vision, the biggest difficulty is finding the pointer. In Windows, the Mouse control panel has a Pointers tab that has several options for changing the color and size of the arrow pointer, the insertion bar, the Select hand, and other pointer icons. It also includes an Animated option that may help draw users' attention to the pointer.

  Also in Windows' Mouse control panel is a Pointer Options tab with several settings that can make the pointer easier to see. The most useful of these is probably "Show location of pointer when I press the Control key." When this is active, pressing Control will shown an animated bull's-eye around the current pointer location. The Control key can be pressed as many times as necessary until the user finds the pointer.

Macintosh systems have a Cursor Size setting. Moving a slider bar increases or decreases the size of the pointer.

- *ToggleKeys.* Most of us, blind or not, accidentally hit the Caps Lock key from time to time, and then find ourselves YELLING IN ALL CAPS. ToggleKeys is a Windows control panel utility that provides a distinctive tone whenever the Caps Lock, Num Lock, or Scroll Lock key is pressed and a different tone when these keys are toggled off.

Solutions within Popular Applications

- *"Zoom" functions.* Microsoft Office has a Zoom feature that can change the magnification level of the document (but not the menu bar or other elements) to anywhere from 10 percent to 500 percent. Because this does not affect the size of the document when it is sent to a printer, it is useful for people with low vision who want to see large text while composing but don't want to reformat it for printing.

  Most Internet browsers now have some type of "zoom" option to change font size. Since Version 7, Internet Explorer has both a Zoom feature (in the lower right corner) and a Text Size option (under the View menu). Be aware that Text Size will work reliably only if the website has been set up correctly by the website developer, while Zoom works regardless of page coding. However, Text Size settings will be used when pages are printed, while Zoom settings will not.

- *Contrast options.* Applications such as browsers and word processors may or may not be responsive to contrast options set through the control panels. It's worth checking the application's documentation to see if it includes options for setting font and background color preferences.

- *Color blindness and proofreading tools.* Microsoft Office programs have an option for underlining misspelled words in red and ungrammatical words and phrases in green. Some people with color-blindness or other visual disabilities will not be able to distinguish between the two types of underlining. Although the colors cannot be modified, right-clicking on any underlined word will bring up contextual help, which should provide sufficient information about whether the issue involves spelling or grammar.

Third-Party Solutions

- *Magnification software.* At a minimum, magnification software does exactly what its name implies: it makes text larger, sometimes by huge orders of magnitude. When evaluating programs, be sure to notice the quality of the magnified text. Some programs make the text look "blocky" and hard to read, while others have sophisticated means of making even highly magnified letters look crisp.

> Making text larger is not always the right access solution. People with tunnel vision caused by glaucoma, diabetic retinopathy, and other conditions lose their peripheral vision but still have usable central vision; the effect is like looking through a paper tube. For these individuals, enlarging text will mean that they can see less information at a time. Therefore, they will likely prefer to see text in standard or even decreased font sizes. The options described for Microsoft Office and browsers permit text reduction as well as enlargement.

Most programs go beyond simply magnifying text by providing options for modifying pointer appearance, changing color contrast, and speaking text. Choose programs that strike a good balance between flexibility and intuitiveness; for example, if the majority of your magnification users will be elders, they may need fewer features and prefer programs with a simpler interface.

- *Screen readers.* Screen readers provide an alternative to the monitor by speaking all information visible on the computer screen plus some information not presented to sighted users, such as a report on the number of links on a website. They also have to substitute for the mouse by providing keyboard commands for controlling the various screen reader features and frequently for interacting with popular programs—for example, commands for moving among form fields on a webpage. If you have refreshable braille hardware, a screen reader is the usual means for providing appropriate software drivers. Screen reader users will need to use headphones to protect their own and others' privacy.

  Windows screen readers have traditionally cost hundreds of dollars. In response, an increasing number of free screen readers are being developed to provide speech output for basic applications—including browsers and word processors, which may be the primary applications the library provides for patrons.

- *Scan/read programs.* These are optical character recognition (OCR) programs that allow any reasonably good quality typeset text—from magazines, books, correspondence, and so on—to be converted into electronic format via a scanner (usually purchased separately). The program then reads the text aloud and allows it to be edited, saved, or exported to a word processor.

  Scan/read programs designed for blind/low vision users and those designed for people with comprehension barriers are distinct in multiple ways:

Programs to Address Monitor Barriers	Programs to Address Comprehension Barriers
• Usually only provide scanning and reading capabilities; may be able to scan and recognize paper money.	• Provide a variety of other features to help with comprehension and writing; versions may even be available that do not include scanning capabilities.
• Provide voice output for menus, dialogue boxes, and other features of the program interface.	• Usually do not speak interface features.
• Have a minimal interface with no graphics.	• Have an interface that includes graphics, which may provide important cues about the purpose of each function.
• Can be used entirely through keyboard commands.	• Generally require some mouse use.

For any program that provides speech output, it's important to ensure that it supports a variety of voice options. This is because some speech output users will have hearing impairments that make some voices easier to hear than others, and others will simply have strong preferences about the type of voice they want to listen to. If the program does not come with a range of voices, check to see if additional voices can be purchased inexpensively and added.

Be aware that large monitors will probably prove to be your most desirable piece of assistive technology among nondisabled individuals, from professionals who are used to having enough monitor space to see multiple documents at once, to kids who think they're fun. Keep this in mind when you're setting fair use policies; for example, if an elder really needs access to the monitor but it's currently being used by a teenager reading small print, your policy could be to ask the latter patron if he or she would move to the next available station with a standard size monitor. Also encourage staff responsible for mainstream purchasing to consider this when selecting new monitors, because even 23″ monitors can now be purchased for under $200.

Keep in mind that it is usually possible (if not optimal) for people with comprehension barriers to use scan/read programs designed to address monitor barriers. However, for most of the reasons listed, a blind person will likely not be able to use the programs designed for people with comprehension barriers. If cost is a major consideration, it's possible that basic OCR software, which is bundled with most scanners, can be satisfactorily accessed via a screen reader.

- *Large monitors.* For people who benefit from large print, larger monitors are essential. Monitors that are wider than they are tall can be particularly useful, because they maximize the percentage of a line of magnified text that users can see at a time.

- *Refreshable braille displays.* Refreshable braille is a technology that uses plastic pins that move up and down to represent braille characters. As the user navigates through a page or a website, the pins change position to reflect the text that is now in focus. Most devices have ways of conveying additional information; for example, the character corresponding to the current location of the pointer may vibrate. They require use of a screen reader to provide an interface between the device and the computer.

  Many braille users strongly prefer braille to speech for accessing computer output. As the American Foundation for the Blind points out: "The advantages of braille displays over synthetic speech are that it [*sic*] provides direct access to information; allows the user to check format, spacing, and spelling; and is quiet" (AFB, 2011). However, braille displays are quite expensive, and you may want to invest in them only if you are sure they will be used. If you are, make sure that your screen reader will support the display you've chosen.

- *Braille printers and braille translation software.* As noted in Chapter 1, only a small percentage of blind people use braille. If you get a braille printer to produce library collaterals such as event announcements, think about whether you want to also make it available to patrons. Look at any usage limit policies you have established for regular printing and whether these should also be applied to braille printing. Keep in mind that braille paper is significantly more expensive than standard printer paper, but braille printers don't incur toner costs.

  Braille printers cannot interpret standard text files, so you will also need a conversion method. An online service called RoboBraille (http://www.robobraille.com/) accepts text files, converts them into audio, DAISY, or printer-ready braille files, and e-mails a link to the converted file; the service is free for noncommercial use. Braille translation software that can be installed on a hard drive is also available.

- *Voice recognition software.* Voice recognition software is often proposed as an input strategy for people with visual disabilities.

While this is enjoying some success on mobile devices, with computers it usually introduces an unnecessary level of complexity. Most people with visual disabilities are able to physically access the standard computer keyboard and can take advantage of keyboard commands as a mouse alternative (see under Mouse Barriers, p. 34).

Additional, and sometimes quite expensive, software is often required to run voice recognition software and screen readers together. Even then, a core problem is not addressed: because of the homonymic nature of language, screen reader users will need to perform letter-by-letter proofreading to determine whether the voice recognition program put up, say, "I can't elope with her" or "Ike antelope wither."

Creative Solutions

Glare on monitor screens will be an access issue for many of your patrons, particularly elders. Flat-panel monitors tend to be more glare-resistant than older CRT monitors. Positioning the monitor perpendicular to a natural light source may also cut down on glare. If neither of these is possible, you can purchase a glare reduction screen and hood that can be installed to block unwanted light. However, you may find that taping cardboard to the sides of the monitor is equally effective and much less expensive.

Keyboard Barriers

No matter how much hype surrounds other types of input strategies, the keyboard persists. Despite attempts to alter the standard design, keyboards look not only much as they did in the early days of personal computing, but they're basically unchanged from the typewriter design of a hundred years ago. These keyboards cause problems for many people with disabilities and can contribute to development of repetitive strain injuries among people who weren't previously disabled.

Issues and Key Strategies

Reasons that individuals might experience keyboard barriers include the following:

- Issue: Inability to use a standard keyboard
  - Strategy: Provide an alternative keyboard.
  - Strategy: Provide an alternate input method, such as an onscreen keyboard.
- Issue: Problems finding the desired key
  - Strategy: Provide a keyboard with the letters in a more familiar order, such as alphabetic.
  - Strategy: Provide a keyboard with large print letters.

The standard layout of alphabetic keys is sometimes thought to have been designed for inefficiency. The explanation, possibly apocryphal, is that in the early days of manual typewriters proficient users would type too fast, causing the typebars to tangle. However, in the years since the invention of electric typewriters and computers, no one seems to have noticed that typebars are no longer used. More efficient layouts have been designed, including the Dvorak, which requires less hand movement for touch typists to reach the most commonly used keys. None of these has ever caught on.

Checklist for Selecting Monitor Access Solutions

Magnification Software

- ❏ What size options are provided for magnifying text?
- ❏ Does magnified text look "blocky" or is it smooth, even at high levels of magnification?
- ❏ Do users have the option of magnifying either the whole screen or selected portions?
- ❏ Does the software allow color contrast to be modified to users' preferences?
- ❏ Does the software have options for making the pointer easier to find?
- ❏ Does the software have a speech output option that can be easily turned on and off? Does the voice sound mechanical or natural? Are there options for reading in multiple languages? Can the voice pitch, speech rate, gender, language, and other factors be adjusted?
- ❏ Is the interface easy to use and uncluttered?
- ❏ Is the documentation straightforward? Is it available in large print and/or electronic formats?

Screen Reader Software

- ❏ Does the voice sound mechanical or natural? Are there options for reading in multiple languages? Can the voice pitch, speech rate, gender, language, and other factors be adjusted?
- ❏ If you are purchasing a refreshable braille device, will the screen reader work with this device?
- ❏ Does the software work with all the mainstream applications the library provides? If not, which ones does it not support?

Scan/Read Software

- ❏ Does the voice sound mechanical or natural? Are there options for reading in multiple languages? Can the voice pitch, speech rate, gender, language, and other factors be adjusted?

Refreshable Braille Devices

- ❏ How many braille cells are on the display?
- ❏ Will it work with your screen reader?
- ❏ Does it have additional pins on the cells for communicating information such as capitalization? Does the cell corresponding to the cursor vibrate?

Braille Printers

- ❏ Can materials be printed on both sides of the page ("interpoint")?
- ❏ What is the print speed?
- ❏ Does the printer require special paper? If so, how expensive is each ream?

- Issue: Problems activating individual keys
  - ○ Strategy: Modify the standard keyboard hardware through control panels or keyguards.
- Issue: Problems activating multiple key combinations (such as Control + Alt + Delete)
  - ○ Strategy: Use the StickyKeys utility built into most operating systems.
- Issue: Slow typing speed
  - ○ Strategy: Provide appropriate word prediction software.
  - ○ Strategy: Take advantage of the AutoCorrect and AutoComplete features in Microsoft Office.

- Issue: Hitting unwanted keys or getting unwanted key repeats
  - Strategy: Use an operating system utility to modify keyboard sensitivity.
- Issue: Inability to hear error tones generated when an incorrect key is pressed
  - Strategy: Have the screen flash at the same time as the tone is played.

Operating System Solutions

- *StickyKeys.* For one-handed typists or those with small hands, the most difficult part of keyboard use is holding down multiple keys when typing capital letters and issuing commands such as Alt + F4 or Command + Q. StickyKeys, a small utility built into all Windows and Macintosh operating systems, allows keys to be pressed in sequence. This means, for example, Windows users who want to press Control + Alt + Delete to bring up the Task Manager can press the Control key, release it, press the Alt key, release it, go off for a ten-course dinner (StickyKeys is not time-dependent), come back, press the Delete key, and have the computer react exactly as if the three keys were held down simultaneously.

- *FilterKeys/Slow Keys.* In some cases, users have problems hitting unwanted keys or key repeats. A utility called "FilterKeys" on Windows computers and "Slow Keys" on the Macintosh helps by increasing the amount of time necessary to press a key before it registers. This is particularly useful for people with cerebral palsy or Parkinson's. FilterKeys can also be used to slow down or prevent key repeats; Slow Keys does not have this capability.

  Make sure that if patrons have access to FilterKeys/Slow Keys there's some way to automatically turn it off between users. Many a nondisabled computer user has complained about a broken keyboard, only to find out that the problem is really FilterKeys/Slow Keys modifying the input speed.

- *Alternative layouts.* It's possible in Windows and Macintosh systems to change the keyboard layout to the more efficient two-handed Dvorak setup, which among other innovations puts all the vowels on the home row. You can also set up a left-hand or right-hand Dvorak layout, designed for one-handed typists; the two layouts are mirror images of each other.

  Keyboards that already have Dvorak labels exist, but they can be unnecessarily expensive. Companies that make large print and braille labels may also have stickers that allow you to relabel a keyboard or two if you have Dvorak users among your patrons. Labels that display both the Dvorak and traditional values for each key are also available.

- *Onscreen keyboard.* This is similar to the virtual keyboard now included in the operating systems of most mobile devices.

Windows operating systems from XP onward include an onscreen keyboard, which can be activated using the mouse or other hardware in one of three modes: direct selection (clicking on a key), dwell (pausing the mouse over a key until it registers), and scanning (waiting until the row with the desired key is highlighted, pressing the mouse button or a switch, and then repeating the scanning process within the row). The keyboard automatically runs its own version of StickyKeys. Starting in Windows 7, this keyboard also includes simple word prediction (see under Third-Party Solutions, p. 31), so that users won't need to type every letter of every word. Macintosh systems also have a basic onscreen keyboard, but it does not have word prediction or StickyKeys capabilities.

- *SoundSentry* and *ShowSounds*. In some situations, the operating system will make a sound to indicate that an incorrect key was pressed or that key entry is disallowed. Deaf and hard of hearing patrons, or any patron sitting at a computer with no audio output capabilities, may be mystified as to what's going on, because they're not hearing the sound. SoundSentry is a Windows utility that flashes part or all of the screen whenever an error sound is made. The same capability is available through a "Flash the screen when an alert sound occurs" option in Macintosh systems.

  ShowSounds is a Windows utility that is supposed to show a visual indicator whenever an application issues a nonerror sound—for example, if the application starts to play music, a caption would appear saying "Music!," or the name of the song, or other appropriate information. Unfortunately, the indicators need to be built into an application by the developer, and this is rarely if ever done.

- *Voice recognition*. Voice recognition software—where a user can dictate text or speak commands to emulate mouse functions—has been a promising but problematic technology for some time. Windows Vista and Windows 7 have a voice recognition program built in, but it is not as powerful or flexible as third-party programs and only supports a single user. Macintosh computers also have built-in voice recognition, but it only provides mouse emulation. (See discussion under Third-Party Solutions, pp. 31–32, about the appropriateness of voice recognition software for library environments.)

Solutions within Popular Applications

The AutoCorrect feature in Microsoft Office applications can be helpful for users who make consistent typing mistakes. For example, if someone always misses typing the second "r" in "terrible," AutoCorrect will automatically fix it. However, it will not help people who make inconsistent errors.

Third-Party Solutions

Because so many software-based solutions are built into operating systems, third-party solutions for keyboard barriers tend to focus on alternative keyboard hardware. Some of these are simple variations on the standard keyboard; others are quite radical.

- *Split keyboards.* Try holding your hands in front of you with your palms facing down. They get tired pretty quickly, right? Yet this is the position that millions of typists use all day, every day.

  Now try holding them in front of you as if you were going to shake hands. This is a more natural position, so it's less fatiguing. An added bonus is that you're less likely to be resting your wrists flat against the keyboard or table, so you're not compressing the channel of bones and ligaments that house the median nerve at the base of the hand—otherwise known as the "carpal tunnel." The easiest way to achieve a natural position when typing is by using a keyboard where the two sides can be angled, either horizontally (allowing the two sides to fan out), vertically (allowing the two sides to slope upward), or both.

  Ergonomic guidelines generally recommend that users' wrists be kept straight but don't dictate that they must be facing the ground. Split keyboards allow users to type by angling their wrists vertically, which is often more comfortable. These keyboards come in two styles: "fixed split," which slope the two sides at a specific angle; and "adjustable split," which allows users to change the horizontal and/or vertical angle of both sides. Some adjustable split keyboards allow users to change the angle of each side separately or even allow the two sides to be separated and positioned entirely independent of each other. Because of their flexibility, adjustable split keyboards are much better options than fixed-split keyboards for public computer labs.

  Select adjustable-split keyboards that strike a good balance between flexibility and sturdiness. While you want a keyboard designed to accommodate as many different people as possible, it won't accommodate anyone if it keeps breaking down.

- *Alphabetic keyboards.* If you already know the alphabet, why bother learning a new letter order for typing? Keyboards where the key layout proceeds from "A" at the top left to "Z" at the bottom right can be useful for people with cognitive disabilities as well as for many elders who never learned to touch type. This layout is also popping up in some mainstream designs for mobile devices.

- *Intellikeys keyboard.* The Intellikeys (Cambium Learning; http://intellitools.com/ProgramPage.aspx?parentId=074003405&functionID=009000008&site=itc) is a unique keyboard that can be customized in an infinite number of ways through the use of overlays that slide in and out. The keyboard comes with a variety of overlays, including an alphabetic one; all of these have

Some patrons may own alternative keyboards and mice that they wish to bring with them and use with the library computers. Consult with your IT staff and develop a policy appropriate to your library—for example, devices must be plugged in and unplugged by staff members, devices must be evaluated by staff on a test computer before they can be approved for use on the public computers, or only devices with a USB interface will be permitted. If you do permit users to plug in their own USB devices, you may need to get a USB hub so they don't have to reach around to the back of the computer.

Carpal tunnel syndrome and other repetitive strain injuries aren't a new phenomenon. They were reported at least as far back as the 1700s by Dr. Bernardino Ramazzini, who wrote, "I knew a Man who, by perpetual writing, began first to complain of an excessive Weariness of his whole right Arm. . . . That he might sustain as little Loss as possible by the Accident, he learn'd to write with his left Hand, which was soon after seiz'd with the same Disorder" (Humanic Ergonomics, 2011). The modern difference is age of onset—it used to be diagnosed primarily in individuals aged 55+, but now it's been seen in children as young as eight (Narain, 2006).

View the word "ergonomic" when used in marketing a keyboard, or any equipment, with healthy skepticism. There is no consumer agency that monitors whether a product design actually follows good ergonomic principles. I've even seen supposedly ergonomic keyboards that force users' wrists into positions almost guaranteed to cause or exacerbate injury.

large keys with high-contrast labels. Custom overlays can also be designed using Cambium's Overlay Maker software, or you can go to the free Activity Exchange website at http://aex.intelli tools.com/ and download overlays that others have created. Libraries have used standard or customized Intellikeys overlays to facilitate access to specific applications or websites, including their online catalogues.

- *One-handed keyboards.* Keyboards designed for one-handed users are available, but these tend to require a significant learning curve and can be disproportionately expensive, especially if you need to purchase both right- and left-handed models. An alternative strategy that also has a learning curve but can have wider benefits for patrons would be to purchase one-hand typing tutorial software or manuals; these teach users how to type one handed on standard keyboards.

- *Onscreen keyboards.* These are similar to the keyboards included with the Windows and Macintosh operating systems but usually have advanced options for configuring layout, word prediction, and so forth. If the built-in onscreen keyboard doesn't meet users' needs, you may want to consider one of these third-party programs.

- *Other alternative keyboards.* Many unusual keyboards not covered by the descriptions here are available. A good guideline, at least for your initial purchases, is to select keyboards that look fairly standard except for one or two features, such as adjustability. Users may be more willing to try out alternative keyboards if they don't look startlingly exotic.

- *Application-specific keyboards.* In a few instances, keyboards are developed for compatibility with specific software programs. For example, some magnification programs now have optional keyboards with large print labels and a row of buttons that provide easy access to the most frequently used program features. These can be very useful, because they minimize the setup time, training curve, and amount of memorization necessary to use a given program.

Other accommodation strategies include the following:

- *Keyguards.* Keyguards are a simple solution that benefit many one- or two-finger typists with hand tremors. These are sheets of Plexiglas or a similar material with holes cut in them in the same configuration as the keyboard keys. When the guard is placed over a keyboard, it helps guide the user's finger to the desired key while preventing accidental key activations. Keyguards are more helpful for some users than the FilterKeys/Slow Keys utilities (discussed earlier).

  Keyguards are not generic; every type of keyboard needs its own specific keyguard. Turning Point Solutions (http://www.turningpointtechnology.com/) has keyguards for many keyboard models in stock or can make a custom one relatively inexpensively.

- *Word prediction.* Word prediction software designed for people who have comprehension barriers (see p. 40) can also help increase typing speed for people who experience keyboard barriers. To accommodate both groups with a single product, select software that can predict phrases as well as single words and that works with most or all of the mainstream applications that the library provides.

- *Wrist rests.* Many people are familiar with foam wrist rests, purported to prevent repetitive strain injuries; few people use them correctly. If you are going to provide these, accompany them with information on correct use—keep your wrists above them when you're typing; rest your wrists lightly on them when you're not.

- *Adhesive large print/braille labels.* One of the sillier things about standard keyboard design is that key labels take up only a small fraction of the key surface. Large print labels, which will be easier for many patrons with low vision to see, are available in a wide range of color combinations—white letters on a black background, black on yellow, black on green, and so forth. The labels generally stay attached even with heavy use. Braille and combination large print/braille labels are also available.

- *Voice recognition software.* Commercially available technology that translates speech into text or mouse commands has been around for nearly 30 years, and it's well known enough that you will probably get at least one request for it from your focus group and interview participants. However, people often know about it only through *Star Trek* or TV ads, neither of which provides the whole picture of its complexity. Voice recognition takes a significant amount of practice and patience to be used efficiently, requires an appropriate computer and environment, and does not work well with all voices.

   If you can provide all of the following in addition to the software, some of your patrons will probably be able to use voice recognition at the library:

   - *A quiet room for patrons to use when dictating.* This ensures that ambient noise will be kept to a minimum and that the privacy of both the person dictating and other patrons will be maintained.
   - *A powerful computer.* Current technology requires at least 4 GB of memory (RAM) and a 2.6 GHz processor to work with any accuracy and will work better if additional memory is provided. System requirements listed on manufacturers' websites are often grossly underestimated, because they don't take into account that other programs, many of which are also memory hogs, will be working at the same time as voice recognition.

Word prediction is becoming a common mainstream feature. Most people have seen Google's capability to anticipate search terms as you type. The popular typing app Swype also has a prediction option; not surprising, because one of Swype's creators, Randy Marsden, has been a long-time leader in the assistive technology field.

White-on-black labels are particularly useful for training labs. I once worked with a computer lab for elders that put these labels on many of their keyboards. People with visual impairments found these adapted keyboards easier to see all the time— and everyone found them more visible when the LCD projector was turned on and lights were turned off.

○ *A USB microphone.* Headsets work best but introduce sanitation issues; library staff should clean the mouthpiece with alcohol wipes between users. Desktop microphones may work for users who cannot or prefer not to put on headsets.

○ *Training assistance.* Voice recognition use is not as intuitive as it seems; for example, users have to speak most or all punctuation and may need to remember to issue different types of commands for different number formats (time, currency, dates, etc.). One strategy that will involve a minimum of staff time is to purchase VoicePower from VoiceTeach, LLC (http://www.voiceteach.com/), a tutorial software package for Dragon NaturallySpeaking, the best-known and most powerful Windows voice recognition product as of this writing. VoicePower also functions as a reference source for using NaturallySpeaking.

Creative Solutions

- Most keyboards have small nubs on the F and J keys so that touch typists can find the home row easily; however, many people have difficulty feeling these. The nubs can be augmented via use of "puffy paint," also known as fabric paint or 3D paint, which is available from most craft stores. This is paint that can be used to create three-dimensional dots as large and high as you wish; it dries quickly and comes in a wide variety of colors. If patrons have difficulty remembering where certain keys are located, puffy paint can also be used for labeling; for example, you can draw a large, tactile "T" on the Tab key.

- Sometimes, people may overcompensate for hand or arm weakness by pressing too hard on the keyboard, constantly moving it out of position. Small strips of hook-and-loop fasteners such as Velcro can be used to anchor keyboards in place while allowing them to be moved when necessary. Non-slip fabric such as Dycem or Rubbermaid shelf liners (available at hardware and discount stores) can also be used; it will hold the keyboard less securely but does not require any permanent adhesion to tables.

Mouse Barriers

For people with cognitive disabilities (as well as brand-new computer users), mouse use can be hard to comprehend, particularly because it's hard to compare it to anything else; what else do you push back and forth on a horizontal surface to make a virtual arrow go vertically up and down on a screen? Individuals with physical disabilities may have problems with moving or clicking the mouse. In addition, because standard mouse use requires good hand–eye coordination, it is impossible for blind people to use, and it may be difficult for people with low vision.

Most mouse operations are accomplished in two steps. First, the user moves the mouse until a pointer (usually in the form of an arrow, hand

An exceptionally useful tool for training new computer users is a free website called Mouserobics (http:// www.ckls.org/~crippel/ computerlab/tutorials/mouse/page1 .html). Mouserobics presents a straightforward, fun, and age-neutral series of exercises for learning how to click on links and form fields. With a minimal amount of practice, I've seen individuals who'd never previously heard of a mouse become proficient within 15 to 30 minutes. Mouserobics has also been translated into a variety of languages, including Spanish, Tagalog, and Finnish.

Checklist for Selecting Keyboard Access Solutions

Hardware

- ❑ Can the solution be adjusted to meet the needs of multiple users?
- ❑ Does the solution provide an alternative strategy that will be of use to multiple users, for example, an alphabetic key layout?
- ❑ How intuitive is the solution?
- ❑ Will the solution stand up well to possible heavy use? Is there a warranty?

Onscreen Keyboard Software

- ❑ Does the program provide significant capabilities beyond the keyboards built into the operating system? If so, what are these?

Word Prediction Software

- ❑ Will the solution work well for people with either physical or cognitive needs?

Voice Recognition Software

- ❑ Can the environmental considerations listed on pages 31–32 be provided (e.g., a sufficiently powerful computer)?
- ❑ Does the software support multiple users?
- ❑ Does the software provide both dictation and mouse emulation functions?

with pointing finger, or vertical line) is positioned where the user wants it. They then click a mouse button to activate an interactive element such as a link or to specify where keyboard input will occur. In most—but not all—applications, this can be carried out successfully regardless of whether a patron is using a standard mouse, moving the pointer via keyboard shortcuts, pressing a touch screen, or speaking commands. The exceptions come when a website or application has been designed to work only with a standard mouse, usually because the designer is unaware of the need for compatibility with other strategies. (See Chapter 4 for further discussion about website compatibility issues.)

Issues and Key Strategies

Areas where patrons might experience mouse barriers include the following:

- Issue: Grasping and moving the mouse
  - Strategy: Provide an alternative mouse that reduces/eliminates the need to grasp.
  - Strategy: Provide an alternative mouse that reduces/eliminates movement by the user's shoulder, arm, or wrist.
- Issue: Accurately moving the cursor to the desired target
  - Strategy: Modify pointer speed and acceleration.
  - Strategy: Use keyboard commands to emulate mouse functions.
- Issue: Clicking the mouse buttons and dragging objects
  - Strategy: Provide an alternative hardware or software means of performing clicking and dragging functions.
  - Strategy: Modify or eliminate double-clicking.

- Issue: Understanding the relationship between mouse movement and onscreen activity
  - Strategy: Provide an alternative mouse that provides a more direct connection between mouse operation and onscreen results.

Operating System Solutions

- *MouseKeys.* Windows and Macintosh operating systems include a utility called "MouseKeys" that permit mouse operations to be controlled from the keypad on the far right side of most keyboards. A typical keypad has the following layout:

NumLock	/	*	→
7	8	9	–
4	5	6	+
1	2	3	Enter
0		Del	

When MouseKeys is active, pressing the "5" key emulates a left mouse click, and pressing "0" is the equivalent of clicking and holding a mouse button prior to dragging. Pressing and holding any of the other number keys moves the cursor in a corresponding direction. For example, pressing the "1" key moves the cursor down and to the left, pressing the "8" key moves the cursor straight up, and pressing "0" and then "9" drags an object up and to the right.

- *Keyboard shortcuts.* Current operating systems have many built-in keyboard shortcuts for emulating mouse functions. For example, in Windows systems, simultaneously pressing the Control and Escape keys brings up the start menu. Some users may wish to use keyboard shortcuts as a full substitute for mouse use; others may wish to memorize a few shortcuts they think they will use most often. Doing an online search for "keyboard shortcuts" plus the name of the operating system you are using should bring up several websites. You may want to print these out and make them available to interested patrons.

- *Eliminating double-clicking.* Double-clicking not only puts a strain on users' index fingers but it can be confusing to patrons unsure when it needs to be used. In recent versions of Windows, a Folder Options control panel includes a "Click Items as Follows" option, which can be set so that desktop icons and other items that usually require double-clicking can be activated with a single click.

- *Voice recognition.* As noted under "Keyboard Barriers," both Windows and Macintosh operating systems have some built-in capabilities for emulating mouse functions via spoken commands. However, both require a quiet environment, and neither supports customization for more than one user.

Solutions within Popular Applications

Many standard applications include keyboard shortcuts. For most Windows programs, pressing the Alt key will move the focus to the menu bar. Sometimes, names of menu items will have an underlined letter; pressing Alt and the corresponding letter key will move the pointer to that item and automatically pull down the submenu. If the name of a submenu item has an underlined letter, pressing Control and that letter will activate the item or bring up a further submenu. It's worth looking at the application documentation to see if it provides a full list of shortcuts.

Third-Party Solutions

A wide variety of alternative mice are available. Some of the modifications are as simple as making the mouse a different size to accommodate small or large hands. Others look nothing like standard mice but perform identical functions. Most of them still require some hand use:

- *Trackballs.* Standard mice require grasping and a significant amount of arm movement, either or both of which may be difficult or painful for many people. Trackballs allow users to move the pointer by twiddling a ball with their fingers or moving it with their palm; these are probably the most common type of alternative mouse used, even by people without dexterity limitations. They come in a variety of sizes and ball locations— sometimes it's located in the center of the device, sometimes at the top, sometimes on the side where it's controlled with the thumb. If possible, provide a few different models for users to choose from.

  As Donald A. Barclay (2000) has pointed out, balls that can be separated from the base tend to disappear. Select trackballs where the ball cannot easily be removed.

- *Joysticks.* Joystick operation is familiar to many people from video game play; they are also the standard control devices for electric wheelchairs. Joysticks can also be useful for pointer control. They can be manipulated using several different types of grasps—for example, by holding the top between two fingers— and can be more intuitive to use than standard mice.

  Joysticks designed for operation by mouth are also available; to click, the user presses a button on top with their tongue. However, these are very expensive, and sanitation becomes an issue for multiple users.

- *Touchpads.* Touchpads are a standard style of mouse on most laptop computers and are often popular among people who can control a single finger well. USB models are available that can be attached to any computer.

- *Touch screens.* Touch screens are becoming an increasingly common type of interface on mainstream mobile products such as tablets and e-readers and for point-of-purchase kiosks. They can be added to standard monitors as well. Touch screens are particularly useful for people with cognitive disabilities or neophyte computer users; because you touch the screen directly over whatever you want to interact with, it can be a highly intuitive interface. Positioning of computer monitors with touch screens is critical, because you want to ensure that users can easily reach the screen without accidentally knocking it backward.

- *Miscellaneous mice.* As with keyboards, some alternative mice are quite odd looking. The same rule of thumb holds here: if users are able to find some familiar-looking element on an alternative mouse, it may be used more frequently and successfully.

Some hardware options are available for people who cannot use their hands at all:

- *Foot-operated mice.* These allow both moving and clicking functions to be done with the feet. Foot mice require good control over at least one foot and can be hard on the ankles, so they generally have a more limited audience than one might expect.

- *Switch interfaces.* One capability included with onscreen keyboards (see under Keyboard Barriers, pp. 27–28 and p. 30) is called scanning. Each row of the keyboard is highlighted in turn; users activate a switch to select the row that has the letter they want. The scanning interface then highlights each key within the row, and the user activates the switch again when the desired key is reached. With practice, and accompanying word prediction capabilities, this can become a surprisingly efficient option for some individuals with physical or cognitive disabilities.

  A plethora of switches are available—some are activated by interrupting a beam of light, some by eyebrow movement, some by exhaling into a tube, and so on. Because of the range of user needs, it would be nearly impossible for libraries to make purchase decisions about switches. However, libraries might provide switch interfaces, which allow users' own switches to be attached to a computer. Switch interfaces are relatively inexpensive and require minimal setup time.

- *Head mice.* These are designed for individuals who cannot use a standard mouse but have reliable movement of some body part, usually their head. An infrared sensor sits atop the computer monitor and translates the movement of a silver-colored dot worn by the user to mouse movement. The higher end models have increased in quality in recent years, but they are expensive and can be hard on the neck. They are also fragile, so if you choose to purchase one, you will probably want to have it set up only on request; fortunately, their setup is fairly easy.

- *Eye gaze systems.* These are similar to head mice but track eye movement. They are currently very expensive, require users to keep their necks quite still, and are primarily designed for people with no other physical capabilities. However, there is ongoing interest in developing eye gaze systems for mainstream applications, such as video games, and this is likely to result in better and far less expensive systems in the future.

Finally, there are some solutions that are primarily software based:

- *Auto clicker software.* This eliminates the need to press the mouse button. The patron uses any standard or alternative mouse to move the cursor and then pauses it over a clickable item or area for an adjustable period of time. The program will then click once and wait for the cursor to be moved to another area before clicking again. The software can also be used to emulate right clicks and click-and-drag functionality.
- *Voice recognition software.* Voice recognition programs usually contain at least a few commands for controlling cursor movement. If you do decide to implement voice recognition software in your library, an important selection criterion should be inclusion of enough commands that it can function effectively as a mouse alternative.

Creative Solutions

Windows users generally locate the mouse buttons by touch while they are looking at the screen. If some patrons find this difficult, you can use puffy paint to draw an "L" and "R" on the respective buttons. You might also put a sticker on the left button to remind users which one they use most often.

Comprehension Barriers

Unlike the other barriers we've covered, comprehension barriers don't involve difficulties accessing a component of the computer system. Instead, they relate to difficulties patrons may have with the basic purpose of using a computer: acquiring and generating information. This may be caused by disability but may also be caused by factors such as a lack of literacy training or limited familiarity with the language in which information is presented.

Issues and Key Strategies

Reasons that patrons might experience comprehension barriers include the following:

Checklist for Selecting Mouse Access Solutions

Hardware

- ❏ Is the mouse reasonably intuitive to use?
- ❏ Will it require extensive setup by each user?
- ❏ Are movable parts such as trackballs hard to remove, to discourage theft?

Voice Recognition

- ❏ Does the program include mouse emulation commands?

- Issue: Low-level reading or writing skills
  - Strategy: Provide tools that help with reading, such as software that provides simultaneous speech output and text highlighting.
  - Strategy: Provide tools that help with writing, such as idea mapping software and word prediction software.
- Issue: Standard color combinations—such as black text on a white background—are hard to read
  - Strategy: Provide options for adjusting color contrast.
- Issue: Inability to interpret information when it is presented in a single mode (e.g., text-only or audio-only)
  - Strategy: Provide strategies that present information in both audio and text form.
- Issue: Difficulty distinguishing between similar-looking letter pairs such as "b" and "d" in some typefaces or in some type sizes
  - Strategy: Provide ways to change the font type and size.
- Issue: Difficulty remembering the spelling or meaning of specific words
  - Strategy: Provide access to spell checkers, homonym checkers, and thesauri.

Operating System Solutions

Although current operating systems don't have features specifically for people facing comprehension barriers, most of the options listed under Monitor Barriers (pp. 20–22) could be helpful in some situations. However, the preferred settings may be quite different. I once worked with a client with information processing disabilities who asked me to set the display default colors to black text on a forest green background. I complied, and she burst into tears; for the first time, she said, she could read onscreen text. Her needs didn't mesh with any accepted guidelines, but the flexibility of the system was able to accommodate her nonetheless.

Solutions within Popular Applications

The Zoom features described under Monitor Barriers (p. 22) can also be useful to people with comprehension barriers. Some people may benefit from word processor formatting options that increase line spacing or provide wider margins.

Word processors may be rich in other useful features. Fonts and font size can usually be changed at will, and there may be options for changing font and background color. Spell checkers can help people who have difficulty with spelling or who are unfamiliar with spelling rules. Microsoft Word goes one step further with its AutoCorrect feature that fixes common misspellings such as "teh" for "the." There may also be a built-in thesaurus and dictionary to help generate more precise or more colorful writing.

Grammar checkers may be included as well. However, these tend to provide unreliable results. For example, in Chapter 6, I wrote, "resources

Because dictionaries are also a helpful cognitive aid for reading, they are included as part of some popular e-book readers. If you are considering acquiring these readers for patron use, consider including the presence of a dictionary as a selection criteria.

are stored on the Internet rather than on individual machines. . . . " The grammar checker wanted to change this to "a resource are stored on the Internet . . . " in blatant violation of subject/verb agreement rules. Checkers may also insist on a single "correct" usage to the potential detriment of originality. If you use a grammar checker on the first chapter of *The World According to Garp*—a classic novel whose author has openly discussed his learning disability—it's impossible not to note how the text would be ruined by many of the suggested changes.

Third-Party Solutions

A variety of commercial software programs designed for people with comprehension barriers provide additional features, any of which may be useful to a given individual. Features within these programs can provide assistance with reading, note taking, or writing. Some of these programs have only one or two features but can interact directly with standard applications. Others may be feature-rich but have their own proprietary capabilities for presenting text files and accessing the Internet. Demonstration versions of these programs can usually be downloaded and tested for a limited number of days or launches. The following is a discussion of common features.

Reading Assistance

- *Scan/read programs.* As discussed on page 23, scan/read programs for blind people and people experiencing comprehension barriers have significantly different setups. However, their basic functions are the same: to transfer printed materials into an electronic format and then allow it to be accessed and manipulated.

  Some programs are available both with and without scanning capability; the latter option may be significantly less expensive. If you wish to provide scanning but are on a tight budget, be aware that most scanners come bundled with some type of OCR software.

- *Text readers.* Text readers use a computer-generated voice to read document text, providing some users with the multimodal output they need. This function is also helpful for proofreading. Interface elements such as menus and toolbars are usually not read, although many users would benefit from this option as well. Like screen readers, in a library setting text readers should be used in conjunction with headphones.

- *Text highlighting.* The program highlights each word in color as it is spoken. It may use a different color to highlight the current line, sentence, or paragraph. This helps users synchronize audio and visual output.

- *Text masking.* Some users need to hide text that's not being read. Masking features block out everything except highlighted text. If this capability is not explicitly included in a program, it is sometimes possible to emulate it by setting the text and background color to the same value.

Because comprehension barriers can manifest in so many different ways, programs that contain a wide range of features will be the best option for most libraries. This will allow patrons to pick and choose what is appropriate for their specific needs.

- *Text conversion.* In recent years, some programs have added the capacity to convert text into audio files. These files can then be transferred to a computer disk or MP3 player and used outside the library. (As of this writing, there is no analogous commercial product that can efficiently convert audio-only files to text.)

- *Formatting.* These settings are likely to be similar to the color and font settings in standard word processors. They may provide additional capacities, such as the ability to control spacing between words. Any of these can make text easier to read.

Note-Taking Assistance

- *Markers.* These allow users to accent text of interest, much like using a highlighter on print books. Users can generally select from multiple highlighter colors to distinguish different tasks— for example, a beginning literacy student might be asked to highlight all verbs in blue and all adjectives in yellow.

- *Outline generator.* Marked text can sometimes be extracted into a separate document to assist with studying. Before doing the extraction, the user may be able to specify how the text is sorted in the separate document; for example, all text highlighted with the same color will be grouped together.

Writing Assistance

- *Word prediction.* When users type a letter, a word prediction window appears with a list of words beginning with that letter. Users can then select the word they want or continue to type until their word appears. Some of these utilities provide phonetic prediction; if the user types "f," words beginning with "ph" will also appear. Because this software can also help people with dexterity disabilities (see p. 31), you may want to choose a stand-alone program that will work with multiple applications and that will meet the needs of both populations.

- *Idea mapping.* Idea mapping tools allow users to quickly jot down ideas and then organize them using either a flowchart or an outline structure. The outline can usually be exported to a word processor to be fleshed into a full document.

- *Spelling checker.* Checkers designed for people with learning disabilities tend to make more educated suggestions about intended words than the checkers in standard word processors. This is particularly true for phonetic spellings such as "naybur." Microsoft Word's only suggestion for this is "nay bur," but specialized checkers will probably provide the more likely alternative "neighbor" as an option.

- *Homophone checker.* These work similarly to spell checkers but help with homophones—words that sound alike but have different spellings or meanings, such as "bear" and "bare." Users can usually review definitions for each homophone to ensure they are using the word they meant.

There are also online resources that can supplement third-party programs. These include reference materials and electronic texts.

- *Reference materials.* Online dictionaries and thesauri are readily available for free. These provide significant advantages over reference books because they can review misspelled words and offer suggestions for the word the user meant.

- *Texts in electronic formats.* A variety of texts are available online for use with assistive technology. Some of these are out of copyright and may be used freely by anyone; others are still copyrighted and may require that the user to submit proof of disability before they can be accessed. A list of resources is included in the bibliography (p. 132). In addition, many newspapers and magazines publish in electronic formats, which may be available at no charge or for a subscription fee.

Creative Solutions

As noted earlier, there is some overlap between solutions for monitor and comprehension barriers. In particular, the magnification, color modification, and simultaneous text highlighting and audio output features in programs for people with low vision may also be useful to people dealing with learning or cognitive disabilities.

Checklist for Selecting Comprehension Solutions

Flexibility

- ❏ Does the software allow background and text colors to be modified to users' preferences?
- ❏ Does the software allow users to choose the font and font size used to display text?
- ❏ Does the software have a speech output option that can be easily turned on and off? Does the voice sound mechanical or natural? Are there options for reading in multiple languages? Can the voice pitch, speech rate, gender, language, and other factors be adjusted?

Features

Which of the following features does the software have?

- ❏ Optical character recognition (OCR) capability
- ❏ Text-to-speech
- ❏ Reading tools—highlighting, masking
- ❏ Ability to convert text to audio formats such as MP3
- ❏ Formatting tools
- ❏ Writing tools—word prediction, idea mapping
- ❏ Proofreading tools—spell checker, homonym checker
- ❏ Note-taking tools—markers, outline generator

Interface

- ❏ Is the purpose and operation of the program easy to understand?
- ❏ Can the program assist with Internet access and e-mail?

Documentation

- ❏ Is the documentation written clearly, using everyday words?
- ❏ Is the documentation comprehensive—does it address all features of the program?
- ❏ Can the documentation be accessed in an electronic format?

Sometimes screen readers (see p. 23) are suggested for people who face comprehension barriers. This is often problematic for a variety of reasons. The screen reader interface is generally minimal and text-only, which will not be useful for people who benefit from graphic cues. Screen readers also tend to read extraneous information, which may be confusing to people who are expecting what they hear and see to be identical. Finally, the quality of the voice used for the speech output, at least by default, is often poorer than for products specifically designed to address comprehension barriers.

Computer Casing Barriers

Individuals with disabilities may have problems seeing or activating buttons on the computer case, such as the on/off switch and the button for opening/closing the CD-ROM drive. The library may or may not permit patrons to operate these buttons. If it does, there are a couple of simple things that can be done to make access easier:

- Buttons are often the same color as the case and therefore difficult to see. The same puffy paint that can make keyboard keys easier to see and feel can be dabbed onto buttons to make them more visible or make them accessible by touch.

- If users are expected or allowed to turn on the computer, monitor, and peripherals themselves, you can plug these devices into a surge protector so that they can all be turned on with a single switch press. Place the surge protector so that it can be reached easily without compromising electrical safety.

Another area where patrons may have difficulty is with plugging in/removing flash drives and inserting/removing CD-ROMs or DVDs. Some creative solutions have been developed to allow these functions to be done independently, but these tend to be highly customized to individual needs. Because helping patrons with these tasks usually takes minimal staff time, it will be easiest to put up signage encouraging patrons to ask staff for assistance.

Workstation Barriers

Regardless of how much assistive technology is on a given computer, it can still be unusable if it's on a table that's too high or low, if the chairs aren't a good fit for the user, or if the ambient lighting is poor. These considerations need to be taken into account as well.

- *Adjustable tables.* Although the Americans with Disabilities Act Accessibility Guidelines (ADAAG) provide specific information on table heights, tables conforming to these guidelines may not meet the needs of many individuals—short-statured people, people who need to work standing up because of back pain, and so forth. Adjustable tables are a practical solution for accommodating a maximal number of patrons.

There are three types of adjustable tables. One type is complicated to adjust and is primarily designed on the assumption that it needs to be set up a single time for a single user; in public environments, this thwarts the purpose of having an adjustable table. The second type can be adjusted more easily but requires use of a crank or other manual means, which can be difficult or impossible to use for some people with disabilities. Finally, there are electric tables that can be adjusted with light pressure, but these are very expensive. If you can't afford electric tables, provide manual-adjust tables and attach signs encouraging patrons to request assistance in moving them up or down. Because these tables may be popular, you may also want to include language about priority use in the signage.

- *Adjustable chairs.* The U.S. Division of Occupational Health and Safety has a useful website at http://dohs.ors.od.nih.gov/ergonomic_chair.htm that lists all the parts of an office chair that should be adjustable. The more of these adjustable parts that can be included in some or all of the computer workstation chairs you purchase, the greater the likelihood the chairs can be modified to comfortably accommodate people who are significantly larger or smaller than average or who have common musculoskeletal issues such as back pain.

- *Lighting.* Ahmet Cakir (1993) found that vision problems, including dry eyes and burning, occurred less frequently when natural light and two-source lighting (indirect light for general purposes and direct lighting on the task) were used and that vision problems were most commonly reported when only direct overhead lighting was used. If your computer workstations can't be adjusted to take advantage of natural lighting, or if people will be using the lab after dark, provide small gooseneck lamps that people can check out and use at any workstation to make the keyboard and the materials they are typing from easier to see.

Peripherals

In some cases, buying a piece of assistive technology isn't sufficient. It may need additional hardware or software to work properly, or it may need additional equipment to make it appropriate for use in your environment. Peripherals to consider may include the following:

- *Scanners.* If materials that patrons want to access are in print format, a scanner and OCR software can be used to convert them into electronic format. Be aware that scanners will work only with printed materials that have reasonably good print quality and text/background contrast. They will not work with handwriting.

If you are purchasing a scanner to work with a particular piece of assistive technology, check that technology's website. It will usually provide information on types of compatible scanners and sometimes even on specific models.

- *Headphones.* Given the significant percentage of assistive technology that includes audio output, you will probably need to keep some headphones on hand to ensure the privacy of both the technology users and your other patrons. Libraries might provide disposable headset covers as a sanitation consideration or purchase inexpensive earbuds and either give them away or sell them at cost. Consider whether your usage policy (see Chapter 1, p. 12) will allow users to bring and use their own headphones.

- *Microphones.* If you implement voice recognition software, or provide video games where voice input is a component, a good microphone is essential. Headset microphones will generally give the best quality input; however, desktop microphones will be preferable for people who can't physically put on a headset. Carefully check the requirements of any software you install to see whether a specific type of microphone is necessary or preferable.

- *Cables.* Scanners, monitors, and other equipment may not come with the cables necessary to attach them to your computers. Check with your vendor to see what types of cables you'll need.

- *Hubs.* Your computer may not have sufficient USB ports to accommodate all the assistive hardware that might be used at one time. Hubs extend the capability by providing extra ports. Make sure you choose hubs that are powerful enough to run your hardware and that the hub has a long enough cord so it is easy to access.

Other Technologies

As you research assistive computer technology, you are likely to run across categories of high- and low-tech products that don't impact computer use but that might be useful to patrons with disabilities within a library environment. These include the following:

- *Amplification systems.* These can be helpful to people who are mildly or moderately hard of hearing, whether or not they use hearing aids. Most of these require users to wear an amplification device. Higher quality systems also include a base unit, which may or may not need to be wired into the library's walls.

- *Reading and writing aids.* For people with visual disabilities, these can include guides that can be positioned over a sheet of paper to indicate where they should write their signature and pens that have a built-in light. People with dexterity disabilities may benefit from being able to use modified pens; these range from pens with wide barrels for an easier grip, available at most office supply stores, to pens that slip over a finger or that have weights to compensate for shaky handwriting. The foam section of some hair curlers can be used to provide a grip for standard pens or for similarly shaped devices such as crochet hooks; these can be purchased at most dollar stores.

Because color contrast can affect legibility for some people with learning disabilities, consider providing sheets of cellophane in a variety of colors. These can be placed over printed pages to quickly adjust contrast for people who find black-on-white hard to read. Craft or art supply stores sell these inexpensively.

- *Fresnel lenses.* Fresnel lenses are thin sheets of plastic that provide a small level of magnification for printed materials. The magnification level can be modified by moving the sheet closer or further from the page. These lenses are often cheap enough that you may want to consider ordering a batch printed with the library's contact information and hand them out as promotional items.

- *CCTVs.* Closed-circuit televisions (CCTVs) allow pages to be placed under a camera and magnified. These are helpful not only for enlarging any type of typeset or handwritten materials but also for making intricate handiwork such as needlepoint or fly-tying easier to see. Because they neither attach to closed-circuit systems nor show television programs, these devices are sometimes more accurately referred to as "video magnifiers."

- *Rollators.* Rollators are the Swiss Army knives of walkers. Besides wheels and grab bars that can help people walk more easily, they also have built-in seats so that people can sit down whenever and wherever necessary and generously sized baskets to help with carrying library books, DVDs, and other materials.

Summary

More and more assistive technology is becoming available, whether built in to operating systems and standard applications or purchased through third-party sources. Knowing basic information about who may need to be accommodated and what options are available is a good starting place. The mission then becomes deciding exactly what accommodations will work best for your library—which we'll look at in Chapter 3.

▶ *Companion Blog*

For resource updates, visit this book's companion blog at http://www.janevincent.com/iceact.

References

AFB (American Foundation for the Blind). 2011. "Refreshable Braille Displays." American Foundation for the Blind. Accessed February 1. http://www.afb.org/ProdBrowseCatResults.asp?CatID-43.

Barclay, Donald A. 2000. *Managing Public-Access Computers*. New York: Neal-Schuman.

Cakir, Ahmet. 1993. "An Investigation on State-of-the-Art and Future Prospects of Lighting Technology in German Office Environments." In *Work with Display Units 92*, edited by Holger Luczak, Ahmet Cakir, and Gisela Cakir, 54–58. New York: Elsevier Science Publishers B.V.

Humanic Ergonomics. 2011. "Bernardino Ramazzini on the Diseases of Writers." Accessed February 1. Humanic Ergonomics. http://www.humanics-es .com/ramazzini.htm.

Meng, Brita. 1990. "With a Little Help from My Mac." *MacWorld* 7 no. 9: 180–188.

Narain, Jaya. 2006. "Eight-Year-Old Text Queen Has Repetitive Strain Injury." *Mail Online*. Last updated June 8. http://www.dailymail.co.uk/news/article -389800/Eight-year-old-text-queen-repetitive-strain-injury.html.

Selecting the Appropriate Solutions for Your Library

The Americans with Disabilities Act (ADA) specifies a need to make all library services accessible, but it does not provide guidelines on specific equipment purchases to meet this need. This is sometimes seen as problematic, because there are no cut-and-dried standards that would automatically measure when accessibility is or is not achieved. In reality, it's advantageous, because it allows libraries to make assistive technology acquisitions based on the needs of their community rather than having to meet an inflexible standard.

Assistive technology selection should follow criteria similar to those used for other public-use library materials. It should be based on identified demand and product quality. Once a wish list has been developed, funding resources will need to be identified, either inside or outside the standard library budget. If funds have been maximally stretched, creative solutions may be possible.

Consideration of desirability, budget, and compatibility will all be necessary for successful assistive technology implementation. Desirability and budget are covered in this chapter; technical compatibility considerations are covered in Chapter 4. It is critical that you read both chapters before making any assistive technology purchases.

Selecting Appropriate Assistive Technology

When selecting assistive technology, there are three ways to begin: start with a wish list, start with a budget, or start with looking at which options will work with your existing technology. While all of these are valid approaches, the wish list is the starting point that will be most closely allied with your user service goals, especially if you are implementing assistive technology for the first time.

This section covers the relevance of existing best practices in collection development to the selection of assistive technology. It also provides suggestions on how to research various products and how to weigh potential hidden costs of free or low-cost options.

Using Good Collection Development Practices

> *[C]ollection development* is the process of meeting the information needs of the people (a service population) in a timely and economical manner using information resources locally held, as well as from other organizations. (Evans, 2000: 15–16)

In 1931, S.R. Ranganathan posited the "Five Laws of Library Science" (Books are for use; Every reader their book; Every book its reader; Save the time of the reader; A library is a growing organism), which are still cited as core principles of library service (Ranganathan, 2006). Reword the principles around the need for assistive technology, and their gist remains relevant:

- *Technology is for use.* In Ranganathan's time, this law was in response to difficulties users had in getting to places where materials were housed and in getting their hands on the books once they got there. While these same issues are still pertinent for individuals with disabilities who want to use library computers, there is a tangential issue that should also be kept in mind: assistive technology use is *never* an end in itself. Instead, it is a means of providing access to mainstream applications or information. In turn, the applications and information are themselves tools for meeting users' actual goals, such as applying for a job, writing a love letter, or researching the life cycle of gorillas.

  As with books, some users will know exactly what assistive technology will meet their needs, some will have ideas based on hearsay rather than experience, and some will have no prior knowledge. It will usually be necessary to supplement subjective input with objective research so you can best determine which options will be most appropriate for your library setting.

  When selecting assistive technology, it may be useful to keep in mind Ranganathan's description of personal service as an inevitable result of the First Law: "[T]he task of the librarian is not to dump down a mass of books and tell readers to help themselves. Nor is it to forcibly feed them on books of *your* choice. It is to help them; and, to help anyone is to co-operate with him in carrying out his own plans and wishes—to help him to help himself" (Ranganathan, 2006: 68).

- *Every user their technology.* Sometimes libraries start assistive technology implementation by addressing the needs of a single group—blind people, say, or elders, or children with learning disabilities. This may work as a short-term strategy but is unlikely to prove appropriate in the long term. Individuals representing other groups are likely to question why they are not being accommodated as well. More broadly, it goes against the concept of libraries as entities working to provide access to their services to as many of their current and potential patrons as they can. It is therefore preferable to create an assistive technology wish list that addresses the needs of a broad audience, even if not every item on the list can be acquired during the first round of implementation.

On the other hand, keep in mind that accommodating literally everyone is an ideal rather than a reachable expectation. There will always be some individuals the library cannot and should not be expected to accommodate. This will be not only because some patrons will need accommodations that are too specialized or too expensive for the library to acquire but also because no matter how carefully you evaluate options, some patrons will prefer products other than the brands the library selects. Chapter 5 (p. 95) discusses how to help these patrons find accommodations outside the library environment when necessary.

- *Every technology its user.* Some assistive technology is more alluring than practical, especially in a public access setting. Avoid the trap of selecting assistive technology just because it's dazzling; it may quickly instead become dusty, and you'll have a hard time proving that anyone's using it. If you can justify wish list items to yourself, it will be easier to justify them to your funding resources and other allies.

  Comments from William Katz on general collection development and Andy Barnett on technology acquisition are highly relevant to assistive technology selection:

  > It is not possible to select a book solely on the basis that it is "good," without a concept of potential readers. You must understand not only why people come into your library but also why they do not. Further, it is imperative to know both what people do or do not find in the library and to what uses they put the information, the recording, the magazine. In other words: Is the library and the materials you have selected for it really of importance to people? (Katz, 1980: 3)

  > Electronic services and resources should be an integral part of the overall service. No part of the library should exist on an island or be divorced from its mission. Technology should not be added for its own sake, because it is cool or because it will be good publicity. It is even a bad idea to add technology as a loss leader. Like everything else the library does, new technology should contribute to the library's stated purpose. Otherwise, acquiring it is sheer technolust. . . . A new format or technology must add to the library's ability to perform its mission or else it should not consume public funding. (Barnett, 2002: 48)

- *Save the time of the user.* Ranganathan (2006: 337) speaks of an "economy of time" that should be optimized for library patrons. There are a number of reasons why assistive technologies may waste patron time—they have too many options (which, especially in a public setting, is sometimes worse than too few), they have a poor interface design, they cause regular crashes, and so on. Selecting well-designed, sturdy assistive technologies might cost more upfront but may represent a significant long-term savings in staff hours needed to address problems and

Ranganathan spends several pages specifically promoting the need for accommodating blind, Deaf, and nonliterate patrons through a Round Table dialogue among several underserved individuals, a psychologist, and the Second Law itself. Although not all the language is respectful by twenty-first-century standards, the heart of this dialogue is still relevant, particularly the psychologist's response when asked what blind people read: "All kinds of things of course. The requirements of the blind do not differ materially from those of others" (Ranganathan, 2006: 138).

mollify patrons. Remember that the user's goal isn't to use assistive technology; it's to get to an application or to information and use it for what he or she really needs. The more transparent assistive technology use can be, the more efficient the process—and the more likely that patrons will return, publicize your services to others, and provide positive feedback during the evaluation process.

- *The need for accommodation is a growing organism.* As Ranganathan (2006: 382) comments, "It is an accepted biological fact that a growing organism alone will survive. An organism which ceases to grow will petrify and perish." If user needs stayed static, then it would be sufficient to implement assistive technology one time. However, this is seldom the case. At the time of this writing, some of the nationwide factors that will influence the need for assistive technology include a plethora of aging boomers and the rising incidence of certain disabling conditions such as diabetes and repetitive strain injuries; these factors will change over time. There may also be needs specific to your community, for example, a high percentage of adults who are beginning readers. Thinking of your assistive technology services as dynamic is likely to make it easier to keep them relevant well into the future.

Identifying Options

> Most individuals trying to identify adaptive technologies tend to do a quick keyword search in a search engine and read the first four or five offerings from the results page to get an idea of what types of adaptations exist and what audience they are best suited to. While this method may work in acquiring some knowledge and understanding of what is the "hottest" topic in a particular genre, it will not, in most cases, provide an understanding of what makes the adaptations tick. (Henley, 2005: 125)

People often think assistive technology is milk. Most of it, however, is soda.

Let's say you're texting with a friend about to visit from out of town. You ask what she likes to drink with dinner, and she replies, "Milk." At most grocery stores, you'll find a few coolers dedicated to milk. Besides differences in fat content and container size, there isn't much variation. The store will usually carry only one brand, and, if you buy it, your guest is unlikely to secretly pour it down the drain just because it's not the brand she drinks at home.

Now let's change her response to "Soda." When you get to a store, you are likely to encounter soda options filling up both sides of an aisle. Besides sugar content and container size, variables will include flavor and caffeination. You will also need to decide whether to purchase a prominent brand name, a less-advertised option, or the generic store brand. And there may be a squabble if you bring home Canada Dry ginger ale when your friend is a Vernors loyalist.

Selecting the Appropriate Solutions for Your Library

Assistive technology, particularly software, tends to be "soda-ish." For example, there are roughly 20 screen readers currently available for blind people, and a simple listing of these will not tell you which is the most popular, the best designed, or the best value, let alone which is being used by the majority of computer-savvy blind people in your community. How can you make decisions without spending an inordinate amount of time doing research?

Before evaluating specific products, decide which types of products are most relevant for your library, using the product categories listed in Chapter 2. This should be based on input from your focus group and interview participants, as well as consideration of information that you've collected about patron demographics.

Next, look at the input from your patrons and community partners for the names of products in each category to either embrace or avoid, based on concrete user experience. Pay particular attention to products that are used successfully in local computer labs run by colleges, senior centers, and similar organizations. You may also want to poll members of appropriate electronic discussion lists (see the bibliography, p. 131, for a list) or other relevant groups for information about their experiences. This should not be the only selection criterion, but it should carry significant weight.

Multiple online resources will lead you to product information. The most database-like of these is Abledata (http://www.abledata.com/), which lists thousands of high-, low-, and no-tech products for people with disabilities. Abledata can be searched by category as well as by product name or manufacturer. Product links will lead you to the manufacturer's website, which will contain more detailed information about features, system requirements, and so on.

Additional resources include the following:

- The Assistive Technology Coalition (http://www.atcoalition.org/) has the goal of making information about access to assistive technology easy and available. Members receive access to articles, news, and webinars on a variety of assistive technology topics, geared toward public computer areas. An Ask the Expert feature allows one-on-one consultation with an assistive technology specialist.

- Several assistive computer technology conferences are held annually across the country; experts in all aspects of the field give presentations, and vendors use these to announce and demonstrate new products. A list of major conferences is included in the bibliography (pp. 131–132).

- Local user groups often share information about new products. A list of user groups for individuals with visual disabilities is available at http://pages.suddenlink.net/jjsha/abcu/vicug .html. Individual libraries may also sponsor user groups; for example, the Washington, DC, public library has Saturday Technology Training Sessions twice a month (see http://sttsdc .blogspot.com/).

► Companion Blog

Relevant information from the information resources, particularly the Accessible Technology Coalition, will be cited in this book's companion blog at http://www.janevincent.com/iceact.

- The Open Source Assistive Technology Software (OATS) website lists several free products, with download links. The website is http://www.oatsoft.org/.
- The following resources regularly provide information about new assistive technology products:
  - Axistive (http://www.axistive.com/)
  - Assistive Technology News (http://www.atechnews.com/)
  - Disability.gov (http://www.disability.gov/technology/news_%26_events)

The Assistive Technology Product Evaluation Worksheet (below) is designed to help you keep track of this phase of research so you can make informed decisions. The worksheet lets you assess each product

Assistive Technology Product Evaluation Worksheet

Note: Items marked with an asterisk can usually be copied from the manufacturer's website.

Date:	Evaluator:

Product Name:

Product Category:

* Product Audience and Function:

* Contact Information for Manufacturer and/or Vendors:

* Product versions and prices:

* Mainstream applications that the product works with:

* System requirements (operating system, RAM, processor speed, video card, etc.):

* Product features:

Product feedback from in-house review:

Product feedback from focus groups/interviews:

Product feedback from other sources (e.g., websites):

Is product a candidate for purchase?   Yes   No

If "yes," are there competing products that are candidates for purchase?

  Yes—use Product Comparison Worksheet   No

based on its features and reviews. Most of the information can be copied from the manufacturer's website.

After you fill out a worksheet for each item, the logical product in each category to put on the wish list may become clear. If not, the Assistive Technology Product Comparison Worksheet (p. 58; discussed further on p. 55) will be useful.

Sample Evaluation Worksheet for Software	
Date: 3/22/12	**Evaluator:** Bunny Watson
Product Name: Read Me First!	
Product Category: Text reader	
* Product Audience and Function: "Read Me First! helps people with learning disabilities by reading text aloud. Just select text within your document, and Read Me First! will speak it in your choice of clear voices."	
* Contact Information for Manufacturer and/or Vendors: Manufacturer: Vapor Software, 1000 Cemetery Lane, Winterwood, CA 99999, (415) 555-0001, www.havingvapors.com (download demo from www.havingvapors.com/try_me). Vendor: Gotta Lotta Software, 16 Parkside Lane, Appleburg, IN 55555, (317) 555-4432, www.gottalottasoftware.com.	
* Product versions and prices: Basic version, $150; version with both English and Spanish voices, $195. (Based on input from Gracie in the literacy program, we want the version that includes Spanish.)	
* Mainstream applications that the product works with: Microsoft Word, NotePad, WordPad. Does not work with the Internet.	
* System requirements (operating system, RAM, processor speed, video card, etc.): 1 GB RAM, Windows 98 or higher, PCI Express or AGI video card.	
* Product features: Highlight tool, choice of five English and three Spanish voices.	
Product feedback from in-house review: No conflicts noted. Tester commented positively on simplicity and clarity of interface.	
Product feedback from focus groups/interviews: The senior center reports using this successfully; the high school and local Computer Access Center use the competing product SpeakEasier instead. Two focus group attendees have used the program and like it; one tried it but chose SpeakEasier because it can also read the Internet.	
Product feedback from other sources (e.g., websites): A conference paper from 2007 compares increases in text comprehension after using both products and found that SpeakEasier had better results.	
Is product a candidate for purchase? [X] Yes No If "yes," are there competing products that are candidates for purchase? [X] Yes—use Product Comparison Worksheet No	

Sample Evaluation Worksheet for Hardware	
Date: 10/2/12	**Evaluator:** Mary Hatch
Product Name: Incredikeyboard	
Product Category: Adjustable keyboard	
* Product Audience and Function: "Incredikeyboard is the perfect ergonomic solution for accommodating or preventing repetitive strain injuries. It can be adjusted in a variety of different ways to accommodate all users in your public lab."	
* Contact Information for Manufacturer and/or Vendors: Manufacturer: IncrediSolutions, 777 Zingy Lane, Greta Grove, MI 55555, (734) 555-9277 No other vendors listed.	
* Product versions and prices: Small version (no number pad), $125; version with number pad, $175.	
* Mainstream applications that the product works with: All	
* System requirements (operating system, RAM, processor speed, video card, etc.): USB port.	
* Product features: Each side of the keyboard (and the keypad, when present) can be adjusted separately.	
Product feedback from in-house review: N/A	
Product feedback from focus groups/interviews: One person requested the Incredikeyboard but hadn't used it, two people requested the competing AdjustaKeys keyboard, and four people requested this type of keyboard but did not mention a specific brand. The community college had a couple of Incredikeyboards and found them hard to adjust. They also commented that the keys seemed to fall off easily.	
Product feedback from other sources (e.g., websites): One positive review; three reviews strongly prefer the AdjustaKeys.	
Is product a candidate for purchase? Yes [X] No If "yes," are there competing products that are candidates for purchase? Yes—use Product Comparison Worksheet No	

Free versus Commercial Software

Librarians must carefully balance high-cost programs that specifically address a library function and low-cost generic programs. They must also compare expensive, powerful programs with lower-performance public-domain programs. The underlying issue is one of adaptability versus standards. The more creative and knowledgeable the librarian, the more options are available. (Farmer, 1993: 54)

When comparing software options, it will be tempting to give disproportionate weight to free programs. However, you may be able to save yourself a significant number of headaches by testing them as you would commercial programs (see Chapter 4), using the following criteria:

- *Flexibility.* Do the free programs have enough options to meet the needs of multiple users? Are these options easy to find and turn on or off? Can users easily assess the relevance of these options to their needs?

- *Complexity.* How difficult is the free program to use? Will the user need to spend a significant amount of time setting it up before each session of computer use?

- *Sturdiness.* Does the free program work as promised? Does it regularly crash the computer or cause other problems?

- *Documentation.* Is product documentation provided? Is it clear and accurate? Does it include a "cheat sheet" that can be given to users?

- *Support.* If there are problems using the program, or if the program appears to negatively affect other computer operations, how easy would it be to get support from the manufacturer? If a problem is identified, does the manufacturer have the resources to fix it in a timely manner? Is the manufacturer upfront on its website or in the product documentation about letting you know whether it can support the program?

Mainstream versus Specialized Software

As noted in Chapter 2, some mainstream products that you already own include accessibility features. Keep in mind, however, that even these features will require some investment of staff time, because they will need to be documented and explained to users. You can minimize this time by searching for documentation within the programs or online. Third parties, particularly colleges and universities, sometimes do a better job of providing this type of documentation than the manufacturers and are often generous about making the information publicly available on the Internet. Make sure, however, that the third-party documentation is relevant to the version of the product you own.

Making the Wish List

Once information on options has been gathered and organized, you will need to decide what goes on your actual wish list. If there are still competing products in a particular category, the Assistive Technology Product Comparison Worksheet (p. 58) is designed to make this step easier by letting you input and compare summary information for competing products. It uses a point system to measure the appropriateness of each candidate. Each criterion receives one point, except for positive input from patrons (two points) and other public computing environments (three points) who've actually used the products. Once the points for each product are tallied, it should be easy to see which product has the most points and is therefore the likely candidate for purchase.

When the library is selecting new mainstream software, you might suggest to the selection team that presence of built-in accessibility features should be considered as part of the evaluation criteria. However, make sure that these features don't automatically trump other considerations. I once worked for a disability agency that had purchased an accessible copier. Buttons were easy to reach for wheelchair users. Information was conveyed via both audio and highly legible panels. And it made really dreadful copies.

Don't worry about the budget just yet. Keep in mind that assistive technology implementation should be an ongoing process, not a one-time event. If there is a unique and desirable product that is too expensive or incompatible with your computer setup at this time, put it on the wish list and defer its purchase until funds can be raised or the technical issue is resolved rather than simply eliminating it from consideration.

If possible, add a wish list item for reserve funding to meet new and appropriate requests. This can eliminate the need to wait until a new budget cycle or to scramble for external funding before making new purchases on a timely basis.

SELECTION AND BUDGETING IN ACTION

Interview with Members of the Contra Costa County (CA) Library Accessibility Committee

The Contra Costa County Library has put a commendable amount of effort into developing a thorough and thoughtful assistive technology strategy. The following representatives of the Accessibility Committee, which meets monthly and includes librarians from multiple branches, IT staff, and administrators, generously agreed to be interviewed about their equipment selection and budgeting process: Megan Brown, Rob Clima, Susan Kantor-Horning, Kathy Middleton, Vickie Sciacca, Susan Weaver, and Gina Worsham.

What sources of information (including your focus groups, if appropriate) did you use to make decisions about your equipment purchases?

Besides the feedback we got from our focus groups, the Accessibility Committee received a tremendous amount of information on the newest trends in assistive technology from BADSL [Bay Area Disability Services Librarians, a local consortium of librarians charged with implementing accessibility] members. The Committee learns about equipment from BADSL by attending their meetings and subscribing to their e-mail list.

Several Accessibility Committee members visited Lynne Cutler, the ADA coordinator of the Oakland Public Library, to receive a tour of the Main Library's services and assistive technologies. The Committee gathered information on sources for future staff training and received a demonstration of the Oakland Public Library's CCTV and Kurzweil software for people with learning disabilities.

All of the Contra Costa County community libraries are now equipped with a "low-tech kit" made up of accessibility tools that were researched by the Committee and recommended by BADSL and focus group members. Each kit contains two wide felt-tip markers, one signature guide [which helps blind people write their signature], and one handheld 3x magnifier.

Additional information came from a variety of other sources:

- Committee members reviewed local community colleges' websites to see what accessible technology they offered.
- Michael Parker from Access Ingenuity [a local assistive technology vendor] and two community members made a presentation to the Accessibility Committee on products for people with visual disabilities.
- Representatives from the Hearing Loss Association of North America – Diablo Valley Chapter recommended a portable hearing loop [technology that helps hard-of-hearing people].
- Committee members attended workshops presented by InFoPeople [a California training initiative] and the East Bay Learning Disability Association.
- Jane Vincent from the Center for Accessible Technology provided input during our meetings.

Was equipment funded as part of the standard budget or through additional funds?

Funding came from both sources:

- The Contra Costa Library provides the funding for the following at all 25 community libraries:
  - Monitor with a 20" screen
  - Large print keyboard
  - Trackball mouse

(Continued)

SELECTION AND BUDGETING IN ACTION *(Continued)*

- ○ Low-tech kit
- ○ Text magnification machines in five libraries
- ○ Books and magazines, e-books, and services. Lafayette's collection is on all kinds of disabilities, and many of the titles were suggested by our group, Special Parents/Special Kids. Antioch carries *ABILITY Magazine*. The downloadable e-books and audiobooks are available in accessible formats. In fact, the California Braille and Talking Book Library provides services available for patrons to download digital audio books through OverDrive, the same vendor as the Library's.
- • The Walnut Creek Library Foundation, with a gift from the Lions Clubs of Walnut Creek, has funded:
  - ○ One CCTV [closed-circuit television, used to magnify printed materials]
  - ○ Magnification software
  - ○ Assistive listening system and ear-worn receivers
  - ○ T-coil loop hearing assistance systems, including a portable unit kept at the children's desk that can be checked out for use in meeting rooms
  - ○ A headphone at the first floor information desk
- • The Friends of the Lafayette Library and Learning Center funded one CCTV.
- • Holders for pictograms (see Chapter 5, p. 85) were funded by location-specific sources:
  - ○ San Ramon Library—funded by a Pacific Library Partnership Easy-Aid Grant
  - ○ Antioch Library—funded by the Friends of the Antioch Library
  - ○ Lafayette Library—funded by the Friends of the Lafayette Library and Learning Center

Did you choose to work with multiple vendors or just one? What influenced this decision?

For the purchases recently made (CCTV, hearing loops, low-tech tools), the Library worked with multiple vendors. County purchasing requires the library to request bids from multiple vendors for purchases over a certain dollar amount. The Automation Department contacted multiple vendors before making purchasing decisions.

How did you create a budget for non-equipment items, such as training?

We didn't create a budget for these items, although library administrators were open to making sure we made progress on library accessibility. The Committee provided staff training through the Library's Staffnet (Intranet) page, which was set up by our Virtual Library staff. Staffnet will continue to provide the common area for us to learn the most recent changes in delivering library services.

Prior to this, individual Committee members identified and shared findings on the types of products and services we might provide for people with varying disabilities. For example, we put together lists of low and high technology products for use by people with developmental, speech, hearing, and vision disabilities.

Included in the County budget are opportunities for accessibility training through InFoPeople workshops and webinars, ALA and CLA [California Library Association] workshops, or other resources. Members and nonmembers of the Accessibility Committee can take advantage of these trainings.

Staff training for library accessibility does not always require a line in the budget and can be accomplished by a variety of means. All staff can be included on internal communications such as Staffnet or e-mail, and small groups and individuals can attend trainings and share a summary with other staff. We hope to have an accessibility-themed All Staff Day in our future, the ultimate training opportunity.

(*Source*: Middleton et al., e-mail communication, December 29, 2010.)

Budgeting

Getting assistive technology into the library's budget is obviously important as a funding strategy. However, it conveys a larger message as well: assistive technology is important to the library's mission and will be considered on an ongoing basis, at least on a par with other services.

Assistive Technology Product Comparison Worksheet			
Date:		**Evaluator:**	
Product Category:			
Criteria	**Product 1**	**Product 2**	**Product 3**
Name			
Price (1 point for lowest price)			
Can the existing library computers support the product? (1 point if yes)			
Does the product support the library's applications? (1 point for each application supported)			
Does the product have standard features [see Ch. 2 description of category]? (1 point for each feature)			
Does the product have unique and desirable features? (1 point for each feature)			
Has the product been recommended by patrons who've used it? (2 points for each feedback)			
Has the product been recommended by community partners or other libraries that have used it? (3 points for each feedback)			
Has the product been requested by name by patrons who have not used it? (1 point for each request)			
Does the product have positive feedback from elsewhere? (1 point for each feedback)			
Total Points			

In their book *Managing Budgets and Finances*, Arlita Hallam and Teresa Dalston (2005) identify eight different types of library budgets. As you start to plan funding for your selected technology, talk to the staff members responsible for the overall budget, find out which types of budgets the library uses, and see how assistive technology can fit in. For example, if the library primarily uses a line-item budget, then the assistive technology items to be funded may need to be spread among multiple line items: software, IT staff time, front-line staff time, marketing, and so on.

Hallam and Dalston (2005) also outline seven potential alternative funding sources, including foundations, friends of the library groups, and endowments, and list a variety of resources for researching these. These may be your initial best bet if your library has an inflexible budget cycle that won't be revised in the near future. When seeking supplemental funding for assistive technology, try looking for resources in two potential

Selecting the Appropriate Solutions for Your Library

Sample Comparison Worksheet			
Date: 12/7/12	**Evaluator:** Marian Paroo		
Product Category: Text reader			
Criteria	**Product 1**	**Product 2**	**Product 3**
Name	Read Me First!	SpeakEasier	
Price (1 point for lowest price)	$195 (Spanish version) [1 pt.]	$270 (Spanish/French/ German version)	
Can the existing library computers support the product? (1 point if yes)	Yes [1 pt.]	Yes [1 pt.]	
Does the product support the library's applications? (1 point for each application supported)	Microsoft Word [1 pt.]	Microsoft Word [1 pt.] Internet Explorer [1 pt.]	
Does the product have standard features [see Ch. 2 description of category]? (1 point for each feature)	Speech interface [1 pt.]	Speech interface [1 pt.] Ability to modify pronunciation of specific words [1 pt.]	
Does the product have unique and desirable features? (1 point for each feature)	Highlighting tool to make selecting text easier [1 pt.]		
Has the product been recommended by patrons who've used it? (2 points for each feedback)	2 patrons [4 pts.]	1 patron [2 pts.]	
Has the product been recommended by community partners or other libraries that have used it? (3 points for each feedback)	1 partner [3 pts.]	2 partners [6 pts.]	
Has the product been requested by name by patrons who have not used it? (1 point for each request)	N/A	N/A	
Does the product have positive feedback from elsewhere? (1 point for each feedback)		1 source [1 pt.]	
Total Points	12	14—goes on Wish List	

focus areas: library initiatives that support underserved populations in general or people with disabilities in particular and disability/aging/ literacy initiatives that work with libraries or public computer labs.

What to Budget For

In *The Complete Library Technology Planner*, John Cohn and Ann Kelsey (2010) identify ten areas that should be considered in technology-related budgets. Six of these are relevant to the implementation of assistive technology:

- *Planning and consulting.* This should take into account staff time spent on in-house preparation for assistive technology implementation. If you decide to hire an outside consultant to provide advice on equipment selection or any other aspect of the implementation process, their fees should be listed in this category as well.

- *Computer hardware and peripheral equipment.* This should cover all costs for tangible equipment, including tax and shipping. Where necessary, it should also cover supplemental items; for example, a scanner may not come with a cable to attach it to the computer, so the cable would need to be a separate purchase.

- *Applications software.* This should cover all costs for software, including tax and shipping if appropriate. If you decide to purchase automatic upgrades for specific software (see Chapter 6), they could be included either here or under ongoing operating/capital costs.

- *Subscription fees.* Some assistive software is available via subscription, involving payment of an annual fee rather than an outright purchase. The budget will need to account for any of these fees.

- *Initial and ongoing training, professional development, and staff support.* This is an important item, addressing staff time for activities such as consultation with information technology (IT) staff (see Chapter 4) and training of front-line staff (see Chapter 5). It's also an expensive one; Andy Barnett (2002: 50) reports that "One early estimate was that a single Internet station consumes $12,000 of library resources (mainly staff time) annually." If there's one category where you want to budget generously, it's this one; better to have less equipment than less user support.

- *Ongoing operating/capital costs.* This may be the most likely place to put your budget for marketing and evaluation. You may have other ongoing costs that do not fit into any of the above categories but that can be itemized here.

Justifying the Budget

In tough economic times, libraries need to make sure every purchase counts for books, journals, e books, and other materials. The same should be true for assistive technology. You may need to provide justification to the library's budget staff or to an external funding source for the value of the purchases you wish to make and the staff time that needs to be allocated.

One bias you may need to counteract is the belief that assistive technology should be a low funding priority because it "serves only a few people." In response, you can discuss the need for ADA compliance, the local demographics of people with disabilities (see Chapter 1, p. 10), and, for many products, a broader need than is generally assumed (see Chapter 2). There are at least two additional counterarguments:

1. *Moving beyond Catch-22.* This is the flip side of the line from *Field of Dreams*: if you don't build it, they won't come, and therefore you will be failing to serve a significant portion of your community. Barbara Mates' comments from 1991 are still relevant today:

   > Most librarians, when asked to make adjustments to their facilities to better serve the disabled, are quick to say, "but there are no disabled people coming into my library, why should I spend the money to make the library more accessible?" This is indeed a "catch-22"–type question which can best be answered by saying, "if there is nothing in your library why should they come?" Someone must take the initiative, and it should be the person trained to disseminate knowledge. (Mates, 1991: 3)

2. *Equitable treatment.* This argument says, "It can be expensive to accommodate people with disabilities, but it's also expensive to accommodate non-disabled people." Susan Daniels, the former Social Security Commissioner for Disability, likes to point out that wheelchair users, such as herself, are thoughtful enough to bring their own seats to public locations; for everyone else, the location has to purchase chairs (Asch, 2001). Since non-disabled people can expect to be accommodated to the greatest extent possible, in an equitable environment people with disabilities should be able to expect the same.

Creative Strategies

Despite best efforts, your budget may not stretch to accommodate all the equipment that you feel is necessary for your initial implementation of assistive technology. Here are some creative strategies worth trying:

- *Find recycled hardware.* Every state is supposed to have at least one assistive technology reuse program; a list of these is available at http://passitoncenter.org/locations/search.aspx. Some of the programs on the list will have searchable databases online; others may require a phone call or even a visit in person. Online flea markets such as eBay, Craigslist, and Freecycle may prove to be resources as well. For anything that involves expenditure of more than a few dollars, make sure that you have the option of returning the equipment at the seller's expense if it doesn't work or isn't as represented.

- *Talk to manufacturers and vendors.* Manufacturers and vendors may have a product that's being discontinued or that they'd like to expose to a wider audience. It's worth contacting them to see if you can get a donation or a discount, especially if there are no other locations in your area where people can try out their products.

- *Work with community partners.* As mentioned in Chapter 1, what can't be done by individual organizations may be possible with collaboration. Talk to your partners about their own wish lists, and see if cooperation is an option.

Working with Assistive Technology Vendors

Once decisions are made about what equipment to buy and the funding is in place, you need to find a purchasing source. Assistive technology is usually sold in one of four ways:

- *Through the manufacturer.* The manufacturer may or may not offer the best price or the best value. However, especially for your first assistive technology purchases, it is useful to look at the manufacturer's website to get a baseline price and, often, to find contact information for local dealers. In some cases, the manufacturer may be the sole source for purchasing specific assistive hardware or software.

- *Through specialized vendors.* Several companies focus on selling assistive hardware and software either specifically targeting elders and people with disabilities or using "ergonomics" as a catchword. They can also be sources for peripherals such as

> In this context, "manufacturer" is used to describe the company that makes a given product, and "vendor" is used for resellers. However, many companies both manufacture their own equipment and are resellers for other manufacturers.

PURCHASING IN ACTION

Working with Assistive Technology Vendors

Lesley Gibbons is a principal at Sterling Adaptives, one of several small assistive technology vendors across the country. She describes her perspective on what she has found makes for successful relationships with libraries:

> Gone are the days of simply placing orders with vendors. Today, wise organizations, individuals, and business owners are building relationships with their vendors to create new synergies and opportunities that help ensure that they are able to offer the best solutions for their own consumers and to grow their client base.
>
> A good assistive technology vendor will:

- support your organization with product information and options prior to finalizing recommendations and ordering ([sometimes] they will provide demonstrations and even loan out trial devices to ensure suitability);
- ensure across the board product compatibility prior to purchasing; and
- provide a single point of contact for any technical difficulties with any of their technology.

Here are some ideas to make the most of your relationships with the vendors you work with:

- Choose local! Choosing a local vendor means you have a partner on hand in your geographical area to provide on-site support, product demonstrations, and a helpful resource as you build on your assistive technology resources.
- Share information about your organization and its goals and objectives with your vendors so they can be responsive to your needs. Creating close relationships can enable vendors to develop the best solutions for you, and if they understand your organization they can help you do things better. Never hesitate to call a vendor to ask for their input on current technologies.
- Save money via a good vendor relationship! Don't assume you will find the best pricing online or direct with the manufacturer. Often you will find that if you work with their local dealer or distributor they will be able to be more flexible with pricing than anything you find online.

(*Source*: Lesley Gibbons, e-mail communication, January 24, 2011, and February 2, 2011.)

headphones and scanners. These companies are listed in the appendix (pp. 121–122).

- *Through mainstream vendors.* A small percentage of assistive technology is distributed through mainstream channels, almost always because it is something that has general appeal (e.g., a mainstream vendor would be unlikely to sell a screen reader or a highly specialized mouse but might well carry a popular voice recognition program or a basic "ergonomic" keyboard). If your library already has a relationship with a trusted mainstream vendor, check with it to see if it carries any of the products on your wish list.

- *Online.* This is becoming an increasingly popular means of selling assistive technology software. After the product has been downloaded and used for a trial period, the buyer can enter a credit card number and immediately receive registration information. This may not be ideal for libraries, however. First, it requires use of a credit card rather than a purchase order or other approved strategies that the library may use to buy equipment. You may need to make an exception to your standard purchasing protocol. Second, you will need to check whether the purchase price includes a manual, a backup disk, or other standard features that would need to be mailed; an extra fee may be charged for these.

Summary

Assistive technology is like any other type of merchandise: some products are good eggs, while others aren't worth shelling out your money. A thoughtful selection process, combined with a holistic budget plan, will increase the likelihood of successful implementation. However, a third factor needs to be considered before any purchases are made: technical compatibility. We'll discuss that in Chapter 4.

> ▶ **Companion Blog**
>
> For resource updates, visit this book's companion blog at http://www.janevincent.com/iceact.

References

Asch, Adrienne, 2001. "Critical Race Theory, Feminism, and Disability: Reflections on Social Justice and Personal Identity." *Ohio State Law Journal* 62, no. 1: 391–424. http://moritzlaw.osu.edu/lawjournal/issues/volume 62/number1/asch.pdf.

Barnett, Andy. 2002. *Libraries, Community, and Technology*. Jefferson, NC: McFarland & Company.

Cohn, John M., and Ann L. Kelsey. 2010. *The Complete Library Technology Planner*. New York: Neal-Schuman.

Evans, G. Edward. 2000. *Developing Library and Information Center Collections*. 4th ed. Englewood, CO: Libraries Unlimited.

Farmer, Lesley S.J. 1993. *When Your Library Budget Is Almost Zero*. Englewood, CO: Libraries Unlimited.

Hallam, Arlita W., and Teresa R. Dalston. 2005. *Managing Budgets and Finances.* New York: Neal-Schuman.

Henley, Jerry. 2005. "Adaptive Technologies." In *Technology for the Rest of Us: A Primer on Computer Technologies for the Low-Tech Librarian*, edited by Nancy Courtney, 123–132. Westport, CT: Libraries Unlimited.

Katz, William A. 1980. *Collection Development: The Selection of Materials for Libraries.* New York: Holt, Rinehart and Winston.

Mates, Barbara T. 1991. *Library Technologies for Visually and Physically Impaired Patrons.* Westport, CT: Meckler.

Ranganathan, S.R. 2006. *The Five Laws of Library Science.* New Delhi: Ess Ess Publications.

Exploring Compatibility with Other Applications

The use of electronic technology, and assistive technology in particular, introduces compatibility considerations previously irrelevant to libraries. No acquisitions librarian has ever identified a book that perfectly addressed the needs of his or her community and then had to think, "I better make sure it'll fit on our shelves." But to be effective, assistive technology must meet a variety of compatibility criteria. First, it has to be compatible with the operating and security systems on the library's existing computers. It then needs to work with the programs whose use it's intended to facilitate: administrative software, files in various formats, and applications such as browsers and word processors. If your library uses a network to allow multiple computers to share resources, it may need to work with that as well.

This chapter covers the range of reasons that compatibility issues may occur. It is intended to give a broad picture rather than delving into technical details. It also covers strategies for addressing these issues: communicating with information technology (IT) staff, testing products before purchase, talking to vendors about possible problem fixes, and accommodating individuals when fixes aren't feasible.

Communicating with IT Staff

> Without system staff protecting the integrity of computer systems, maintaining hardware and software, and planning for future improvements, there soon would be little in the way of computer resources for library users to access. On the other hand, without public-service staff advocating for the rights and needs of all users, the systems department can easily become the tail that wags the dog: a bureaucratic entity that grinds along for its own sake rather than working for those it is supposed to serve. (Barclay, 2000: 104)

In conflict resolution training, there's a classic exercise called the Ugli Orange. Two participants each receive instructions that they must argue the right of their pharmaceutical company to purchase a supply of Ugli Oranges, an exceedingly rare fruit. One is told the company needs the

COMMUNICATION WITH IT STAFF IN ACTION

Free Library of Philadelphia

Nancy Laskowski is the former Chief of Access Services at the Free Library of Philadelphia (PA), where she oversaw the implementation of accessible workstations in eight branches.

In response to my queries about her experiences and thoughts about working with IT staff, she kindly provided the following.

I worked with the staff members of the IT division of the Free Library of Philadelphia to make the Public Access Technology Workstations conform to the standards which govern all the rest of the public access computers in the Free Library. When I left the position of head of the Access Services Division, we were in the process of testing the adaptive software for compatibility with our public domain (Active Directory), using an outside firm to develop a prototype. Cooperation with the Free Library Tech Support group and their requirements was part of this process.

I have lots of experience working with the Library's IT division, most of it positive. That's partly because I had worked in the IT division for many years and knew which techs would be most helpful and understanding and enlisted their help in working out the details. I also had a good working relationship with the head of the IT division and could beg for help when needed to move things along.

Before I left, we had been talking about setting up a pilot to test how the Access Tech [AT] workstations could be integrated somewhat into the EnvisionWare PC Reservation system. The tech folks thought it would not be a problem, but I had to table the PC Reservation pilot until we had the new workstation configuration worked out. So, that aspect is pending.

For situations where a librarian in charge of AT implementation doesn't have the relationship with IT that I did: I'd say to get the buy-in of someone in the organization who has the authority/power to get IT to pay attention—a "project champion," if you will. If the librarian in charge of AT has clear responsibilities that are part of the organization's short- and long-term plans, that shouldn't be too difficult.

Then there should be very clear goals and a good project plan. (I say "project" because breaking down the operation/program into manageable chunks, with a beginning, middle, and end, gives the best chance for success and satisfaction.) If possible, explain how the AT program integration will benefit the IT folks, as well as the public being served. If there is separate funding for the AT program, and the IT unit will not have to pay for it, that's something to point out. If IT has to support the program without separate funding, that needs to be addressed and factored into the efforts and time-line. It's my experience that if the IT people know what the desired end-result is, and that they are included in all the planning as partners, they can be real allies. Defer to the expertise of the IT staff members and be respectful of the competing demands on their time and resources. Follow up face-to-face meetings with written summaries of discussion points and always have "next steps" and estimated completion dates. Send these summaries to the team and CC (carbon copy) appropriate administrators. Keep the momentum going by following up on progress and by setting up a next meeting date. Just good management stuff!

In my specific experience, when I knew that I had to upgrade the AT workstations, I met with my supervisors and the head of IT to lay out the issues. Together we decided that we didn't have the resources—personnel and time—to do this ourselves. So the IT director suggested we go with an outside consultant to develop the prototype. I had to collect all our licensing information (a bit scattered), then determine what software should be added. Our current AT workstations were not integrated into the Library's network and that was a goal. By integrating into the network, we would have the same security and upgrades available to the rest of the system's public PCs—the Free Library has been on a leased hardware rotation for several years. So the software upgrades for us coincided with the replacement of leased four-year-old PCs. My plan was to upgrade software versions only when new hardware was installed, unless there were critical updates. We discussed this with IT staff and planned to test any critical patches and such before permanent changes would be made.

I wish I could say that I was more "strategic" in how I approached all this, but it was a sometimes painful learning experience. Communication, as always, was critical. Listening, clear speaking, respect, empathy, patience, persistence, judicious use of humor, and, VERY rarely taking off the kid gloves—all essentials.

(*Source*: Nancy Laskowski, e-mail communication, August 10, 2010, and August 12, 2010.)

oranges to make a vaccine that counteracts the prenatal effects of a rubella-like disease; the other is told the company needs them to develop a vapor that can neutralize leaking nerve gas. If the participants are savvy enough to listen to each other while making their cases, they will eventually realize that the vaccine requires only the oranges' juice while the vapor requires only the rind.

Discussions among public service and IT staff will benefit from the same mutual willingness to listen. This can be facilitated by creating or reinforcing a strong working relationship between IT staff and staff responsible for implementing assistive technology. In my experience, IT staff members usually become highly enthusiastic supporters of assistive technology implementation once they understand its purpose—often because they have a loved one who could benefit from the programs under consideration or simply because it presents an interesting challenge. A good starting place may be to invite them to assistive technology trainings provided for front-line staff.

Keep in mind, though, that communication needs to be bidirectional. As Donald A. Barclay (2000) suggests, as many as possible of the staff members communicating with IT personnel about assistive technology need to have enough knowledge about computers to understand what IT is saying and not be afraid to ask questions when something isn't clear. This will not only promote a positive relationship, it will also help staff to understand the underlying rationale when IT says that a particular request is unfeasible for technical or other reasons and communicate this to the patrons or administrators who have a vested interest in the request.

Once communication is established, involve IT staff in any assistive technology-related discussions about access to operating system utilities, acquisition and installation of third-party options (including freeware), and potential obstacles such as networks. Then stay in touch with them to ensure they involve you in relevant conversations as well, particularly discussions of operating system upgrades, implementation or changes to networks, and other systemic changes.

Potential Hardware Compatibility Issues

If assistive hardware is incompatible with your library's computers, it is usually for one of two reasons:

1. The hardware needs a different driver—a small software program that interfaces between the computer and hardware—so that it will work with the operating system. This can usually be solved by downloading the appropriate driver from the manufacturer's website.

2. Occasionally, hardware cannot be plugged in because it has an older style connector, such as the round PS/2 (Windows) or ADB (Macintosh) plugs rather than the flat USB plugs in near-universal use today. Before purchasing hardware, confirm the connector type; if it's not USB, ask if there are known compatibility issues.

If you are planning to add new mainstream applications to your library computers after implementing assistive technology, compatibility with existing adaptations should be an important consideration, but not necessarily an overriding one. Fortunately, the applications that tend to be most compatible with assistive technology will also tend to be the most desirable purchases for other reasons—they may be the applications already most familiar to patrons with and without disabilities, they may be the most affordable, they may be the easiest to obtain via the library's authorized vendors, and so on.

You may be able to use an adapter, available from electronic stores or online sources, to make the hardware compatible. As B. Douglas Blansit (2011: 97) notes in his thorough review of hardware connectors: "A basic knowledge of the types of computer receptacles aids greatly in determining what new equipment may be added to a computer, in moving the computer (with disconnecting and reconnecting the wires), in troubleshooting connections, and in talking with technical support."

Potential Software Compatibility Issues

When you did research on specific assistive technologies (see Chapter 3), you probably found information on system requirements to help figure out whether your computers' systems would support the technology being considered. Once you've confirmed this level of compatibility, your next task is to see if the programs will work with the computers and applications your patrons need to access.

This section is an overview of why incompatibilities may occur. Its primary intent is to help you communicate with your IT staff colleagues and with product developers to analyze and potentially resolve these issues.

Compatibility Issues with Operating System Solutions

Many security systems for library computers prohibit access by default to control panel utilities and other useful operating system options for making the computer accessible (see discussions of these system options in Chapter 2, pp. 20–42). This is one area where bending the rules in favor of public access would seem to be a no-brainer, but even assistive technology can be put to nefarious purposes. I once had a young client gleefully offer to show me how he liked to use the Windows Display settings to change text and background to the same color so that his school's library staff would find themselves staring at what appeared to be a blank screen with no clue as to the cause of the problem. More innocently, a patron in a public computer lab may neglect to turn off the FilterKeys utility, which slows down key acceptance for the benefit of users with dexterity disabilities. A subsequent user may be mystified as to why he or she is pressing keys but nothing seems to be happening.

To counteract this, the library's IT staff probably has a firm policy that all computers need to have their default settings restored between users. Usually, this will also involve restoring the settings of any applications that were used, including assistive technologies. This is part of the justification for assistive technology users receiving extra computer time; much of this time may be swallowed by having to reestablish their preferred settings.

You will likely need to have an extended discussion, or series of discussions, with your library's IT staff to find an appropriate solution that is within the boundaries of both technical feasibility and established policy. Options may include the following:

- Permitting access to some or all relevant built-in utilities on specific computers, usually those that have other assistive technology loaded
- Making built-in utilities available as options via the same library software interface that allows users to select other applications
- Having a staff member temporarily change security permissions when access to built-in utilities is requested

Compatibility When Mainstream Applications Are Accessed through a Hard Drive

Traditionally, both mainstream applications and assistive software have been installed on each library computer's hard drive. However, this model is changing in some arenas, thanks to use of technologies such as networks and flash drives. If installing both the assistive and mainstream technologies on a hard drive turns out to be the least problematic option, but this is no longer the library's standard, you may want to talk to IT staff about continuing to use hard drive installations for one or two computers designated specifically for use by patrons with disabilities.

There is generally a significant, if not 100 percent, congruence between applications that libraries are most likely to make available and those that assistive technology is most likely to work with. These include word processors, browsers, and sometimes spreadsheets or e-mail programs. The more widely used an application is, the more likely it is to present few or no compatibility issues with assistive technology.

Be aware, however, that even standard applications may pose issues if their design changes. Browsers are notorious for varying significantly between version releases. And by replacing the familiar, straightforward menus from Word and other Office programs with an elaborate "ribbon" interface in a 2007 release, even Microsoft proved that there was nothing sacred about long-time product designs.

Assistive technology manufacturers tend to quickly address compatibility issues with new mainstream releases, recognizing that these will affect a large number of users. It's always worth checking the support section of their websites to see if there is any information about known conflicts with specific mainstream programs or program versions. If there is, they may post a patch—a small, usually free piece of code that can be downloaded and added to your existing assistive technology software to make it work with new versions of mainstream software. Patches in the form of new drivers may also be available for assistive hardware.

Compatibility When Mainstream Applications Are Accessed through a Network

In some cases, libraries use network connections to permit resources to be shared among computers within a single branch or across multiple branches. What happens if your library's mainstream applications are

Use of security software may also prevent information necessary for some third-party assistive technologies to function effectively from being saved. One example is voice recognition technology, which needs to create an individual voice profile for each user that is then refined with practice. If these profiles cannot be stored between user sessions, either on the computer hard drive or on the user's own USB drive, then voice recognition will not be appropriate for your library.

provided via a network, but the assistive technology is stored on a hard drive? The answer varies. Some pieces of assistive technology will work fine, others will have difficulty working properly, and others may refuse to work at all. Try asking the assistive technology manufacturer if there are known successes or problems with this type of setup; if it can't guarantee the result, you will need to talk to your library's IT contacts about arranging a test.

Assistive technology may also be run via a network. For example, some developers will sell a site license for five networked copies of their software. This means that up to five patrons at any library branch connected to the network can use the assistive technology at a given time on any computer; the sixth will need to wait until one of the other users signs off. Again, there may or may not be compatibility issues, whether the mainstream technology is also on the network or is on the hard drive; this can be addressed through talking to the manufacturer or testing.

Compatibility When Mainstream Applications Are Accessed through the Internet

Many current applications are run from the Internet instead of a hard drive. Examples include Google Docs and the free versions of Microsoft Office 2010. Because these applications, and the files they generate, can be accessed from any computer, their use has some positive implications. For example, when nondisabled patrons need to yield an accessible computer to a person with disabilities, they can quickly resume their work at any other machine without needing to save their file to a flash drive or other external media. The downside is that the sophistication that drives these Internet applications may also make them incompatible or difficult to use with assistive technologies. Testing will likely be needed to determine whether these applications will work with the assistive technology you are considering for purchase.

Compatibility with Library Software

Some software is marketed to be purchased solely or primarily by libraries and other public computer sites. This includes administrative software, which controls functions such as allowing users to reserve computer time, and security software, which heads off malicious or accidental threats to the computer setup. It also includes online information resources such as databases.

In addition to issues similar to those described for other types of applications, library software may present distinct challenges. For example, a sign-in system may prompt patrons to enter their ID number before using the computer. If patrons with disabilities can access their preferred assistive technology only after signing in, they won't know when the prompt appears, nor will they be able to respond appropriately.

A study by Jennifer Tatomir and Joan Durrance (2010) tested 32 library databases and found that almost three-fourths of them posed some accessibility barriers. Adina Mulliken from Syracuse University and Debra Riley-Huff from the University of Mississippi have been creating a website that tracks accessibility issues found with specific applications. At present, it covers electronic information resources; plans are to expand it to cover other types of library software and to present it in a more accessible format. As the site develops, and more librarians contribute information, it will become increasingly valuable in reducing the amount of in-house testing that any single library will need to perform. The website is currently at http://ascla.ala.org/toolkit/index.php?title= Accessibility_to_Library_Databases_and_Other_Online_Library_Resources _for_People_with_Disabilities.

File Compatibility

Accessibility of file formats is a tangential topic to software accessibility. It is possible to have an application that can be fully utilized via assistive technology and then attempt to use it to open a inaccessible file found on the Internet or brought in on portable media. While the library will have no control over how these files are created, the following sections discuss some basic strategies for making them accessible.

There are two broad categories of files that have long had the potential to cause accessibility problems: documents, which may be in a variety of different formats, and websites, which are basically files displayed via a browser. Newer types of files that are primarily used on portable devices, such as e-books, are also likely to present issues.

The library itself can use a number of best practices when generating files that will be accessed by assistive technology users. A list of resources for these practices is available in the bibliography (pp. 131–132).

Documents

Most assistive technologies work fine with standard word processing file formats. The primary exception is the PDF format; depending on how they PDF files were created, access to them can range from effortless to impossible. If you are getting complaints from patrons about PDF inaccessibility, one strategy is to suggest they print out short files and give them access to a scanner (see Chapter 2, pp. 43–44) to reconvert the printouts into a more accessible electronic format, such as DOC or DOCX (the standard Microsoft Word formats). Another option is to use Adobe's free online PDF-to-text conversion utility at http://access .adobe.com/access/, which works for some but not all files.

Access to other kind of files, for example, spreadsheets, may depend on whether the assistive technology is designed to work with those file types. You may want to make support for these file formats a criterion in your assistive technology selection process. It may also be satisfactory in some cases to export information from these files into a word processing format that is known to work with specific assistive technologies.

Websites

When websites are inaccessible to people with disabilities, it's usually for one of two reasons. First of all, code that is present or absent may affect the operation of assistive technologies. For example, pages need to

One frequent issue with library automation software is figuring out how to let patrons with disabilities sign up for two-hour blocks of computer use instead of only one. There are different solutions to this; for example, the Oakland Public Library has a method that lets authorized users sign back in after an hour as a different user (unfortunately wiping out any assistive technology settings they've just worked to establish), while the Berkeley Public Library restricts use of certain machines to individuals with disabilities.

include a tiny bit of code indicating the primary language used on the page. This might seem superfluous, except to blind web surfers whose screen reading technology is trying to use English pronunciation rules for a page that's actually in Spanish.

The other reason for inaccessibility has to do with design. Guidelines for accessibility have a great deal of overlap with general usability guidelines, as well as with common sense. A good example comes from back in the early days of the Internet, when it was relatively common to encounter websites that used yellow text on a lime green background. This presented significant reading barriers for people with visual or cognitive disabilities. And, frankly, it wasn't all that pleasant for anybody else. Over time, this has changed so that most websites provide reasonable, if not necessarily optimal, color schemes. Other accessibility/usability guidelines cover topics such as putting key information in consistent, predictable locations on your pages and making sure that users aren't unexpectedly redirected from the page they're on.

Reports on website accessibility consistently find a high percentage of problems; for example, a survey of Australian government sites found a failure rate as high as 83 percent for implementation of some critical accessibility features, usually due to coding issues (Usability One, 2009). An interesting solution to this is provided by IBM's Social Accessibility project, which lets screen reader users submit complaints about a specific page so it can be patched on the fly by a volunteer somewhere else in the world. Anyone can use the Social Accessibility site by going to http://sa.watson.ibm.com/account/login_guest, although it's unclear at this time whether the project is meeting the stated goal of requiring most users to wait only a few minutes before fixes are made. A less immediate strategy is the Fix the Web site, which lets users report accessibility problems to volunteer technicians, who then take up the issue with the website developer. Fix the Web is at http://fixtheweb.net/.

E-books and E-readers

As far back as 2006, David Rothman described the variety of different e-book formats as "the tower of e-Babel," and things have only gotten more complicated since (Rothman, 2006). Wikipedia (2011) cites no fewer than 30 different e-book formats, some of which will run on almost any player but many of which are proprietary. Ken Petri of the Ohio State University Library has bravely taken on the task of researching which of these formats are accessible; a podcast where he summarizes a variety of issues is available at http://www.libraries.wright.edu/noshelfrequired/?p=1553.

Two e-book formats are particularly worth noting for their accessibility implications:

- Blio is an e-book format released in 2010 that attempts to provide the same level of standardization for e-books that PDF provides for text files. As of March 2011, Blio files should work with all screen readers (*Blind Bargains*, 2011).

- The DAISY format is designed specifically to promote accessibility. Actually, it's a collection of interrelated formats; a DAISY

> ▶ **Companion Blog**

Information about new or updated web accessibility guidelines will be tracked in this book's companion blog at http://www.janevincent.com/iceact.

Barriers aren't always about technology; sometimes they're about politics. When the Kindle 2 was released, it was fully capable of reading books aloud. The Authors Guild quickly objected, claiming this would cut into audio book profits. The initial result was that Amazon permitted publishers to decide whether or not their books could work with Kindle's audio feature (Nosowitz, 2009). However, initiatives for people who can't use standard print spoke up, and The Authors Guild (2010) has agreed to work with them to ensure fair use.

file contains text, audio, and images and will eventually contain video as well. These formats may be accessed individually or in combination so that it's easy for someone with a learning or visual disability to get simultaneous text and audio access without requiring additional assistive technology. DAISY file coding also facilitates navigation through any of these formats so that users can move to specific portions of the e-book, such as chapters or paragraphs, and bookmark where they leave off.

Dedicated e-readers may also present accessibility issues, and there have been efforts to address this, primarily for the Kindle, which as of this writing is the only dedicated e-reader with speech output capabilities (Ken Petri, e-mail communication, February 23, 2011). While primary Kindle competitors such as the Nook, Kobo, and Sony Reader don't yet have text-to-speech capabilities, they do support use of apps, which holds promise for future developments (Tobias and Vincent, 2011). Origin Instruments (http://www.orin.com/) has developed the PageBot, which will let individuals with severe dexterity disabilities turn pages on a Kindle by pressing a switch.

Litigation is also playing a role in driving e-reader accessibility. In early 2010, Arizona State University settled a lawsuit filed by the National Federation of the Blind and the American Council of the Blind, complaining that all ASU students are required to use Kindles even though they are not accessible to blind individuals. In response, Amazon quickly introduced new accessibility features, even though it wasn't a party in the lawsuit (El-Rahmin, 2010).

Compatibility with Other Assistive Technology

A model used at several libraries is to designate one or two computers where all assistive technology will be installed. This has many benefits— for example, it facilitates the ability of individuals with disabilities to sign up for a particular computer that meets their needs. One potential drawback, however, is that a small number of assistive technologies may clash with each other, even if they are not running at the same time. This can be particularly true if more than one program uses speech output.

If you are going to install multiple pieces of assistive technology with similar features on a given computer, it's worth looking at the manufacturer's website or talking to the manufacturer about known conflicts. Often, this can be solved by something as simple as installing two pieces of software in a particular order.

Identifying and Addressing Compatibility Issues

Just as there is no escaping technology, there is no escaping its negative effects. Libraries will continue to adopt new technology, often before it becomes mainstream. Each new technology will

> ▶ **Companion Blog**
>
> Information about changes in e-book and e-reader compatibility will be tracked in this book's companion blog at http://www.janevincent.com/iceact.

bring a string of unintended effects, which will cause small-scale havoc on staff and patrons.... But if we are careful, if we think clearly about how technology works and if we are realistic about the limits of library staff and patrons, we can foresee the worst of the effects and ameliorate them. (Barnett, 2002: 134)

A thorough review of assistive technology compatibility usually requires at least a three-step process: communication with your IT colleagues, testing for compatibility or reviewing the results of others' tests, and interpreting the testing results. A fourth step, particularly if testing results are inconclusive, will involve talking to the manufacturer of the mainstream or assistive technology or possibly both.

This may seem like a great deal of effort. However, you should consider whether the time you commit up front will be worth the results: reasonable assurance that technology will work correctly before it is paid for, IT staff who feel they have had an appropriate opportunity to provide input and to ensure their job is not significantly complicated or altered by the presence of assistive technology, and above all patrons who have as smooth an experience as possible with using your equipment, requiring minimal staff support and troubleshooting.

Testing for Compatibility

Commercial assistive technology developers generally provide compatibility information on their website or in other marketing materials or are happy to talk with you by phone or e-mail. This information usually covers operating systems, popular applications such as Microsoft Word, and common file formats such as PDF that their products are designed to work with. They may also provide information about network compatibility. There is likely to be little or no information, however, about their compatibility with library software, specific websites, or less commonly used file formats or applications. If you are using assistive technology freeware, there may be no compatibility documentation at all. Therefore, you will likely need to do your own testing to identify and attempt to resolve any conflicts between the assistive and mainstream technologies or between the assistive technology and other variables such as the operating system or the network.

Ideally, you will be able to set up a testing workstation in the library and invite patrons to try out various combinations of assistive and mainstream technologies. In most cases, you can download or order a free demonstration version of assistive technology software and make it available for at least a few weeks. If you need more time, it's worth contacting the assistive technology manufacturer and requesting an extension of the standard demo period, which is usually 30 days.

If in-house testing is not possible or practical, try turning to your community partners and see if they will let you test products on their machines. In this case, find out as much as you can about their computers—operating system, memory, and so forth—in advance so that you can compare their setup to your own. If it varies significantly, testing on their machines may not provide a satisfactory picture of what will happen on yours.

Recruit existing assistive technology users (focus group members, people who have registered for disability services, etc.) to test the mainstream products and report any problems they find. The reporting forms on pages 76 and 77 are samples; you will want to create your own that is specific to the software you are testing. The general idea is to develop a task list covering critical features of the mainstream software and then see if an assistive technology user can perform these tasks independently. Common tasks include:

- Logging in
- Selection (e.g., choosing a desired application from a startup menu)
- Accessing interface elements such as menus, taskbars, and ribbons
- Accessing the primary program function (e.g., the text area in a word processing application)
- Interacting with dialog boxes
- Logging out

At a minimum, testers should be looking out for compliance with four principles:

1. *Perceivable.* Can assistive technology effectively communicate to the user what is occurring? For example, does it let users know when they are being prompted to enter their ID number to log in?
2. *Operable.* Can assistive technology allow the user to interact in all ways necessary to use the mainstream software? For example, if there is a menu bar, can users navigate to it and activate the option of their choice?
3. *Understandable.* Will the assistive technology user be able to understand the program's instructions? For example, if the program says, "Click the green button to continue," is there any redundancy that makes this meaningful to screen reader users?
4. *Robust.* Does the assistive technology and/or the mainstream software consistently crash or otherwise malfunction when a particular action is taken?

Each assistive technology tester should work with an assistant—possibly a staff member—who can provide feedback when barriers are encountered and help bypass problem areas. If the tester is unable to fill out the report, the assistant can help with this as well.

These POUR principles (Perceivable, Operable, Understandable, Robust) are part of the organizational structure used for WCAG 2.0, the latest version of the World Wide Web Consortium (W3C) web accessibility guidelines. They can be a useful framework in many situations for thinking about where accessibility barriers are most likely to occur. A good discussion of these principles is available from WebAIM, a comprehensive resource on website accessibility, at http://webaim.org/articles/pour/#principles.

Communicating with Manufacturers

When problems are found, it may be difficult to figure out why they are happening. Are they caused by the operating system, the mainstream software, the assistive software, the network, or some other factor? Your best chance for finding a solution may be to talk to representatives from the product manufacturers.

Sample Completed Assistive Technology Report Form #1

(*Note*: This sample is deliberately designed with minimal formatting to optimize compatibility with assistive technologies.)

Date: 3/15/2012
Tester: Rupert Giles
Assistive Technology: Speak It To Me screen reader
Application: WordUp word processor

Task 1. Opening the application

No difficulties noted.

Task 2. Navigating the menu bar

Tester reported that standard Speak It To Me commands did not work for navigating among different menus. Once the assistant selected a menu, the tester was able to successfully navigate through menu subtopics and select a desired function.

Task 3. Typing a letter

No difficulties noted.

Task 4. Saving the file

Tester tried using the WordUp keyboard shortcut for saving a file, Alt + S. This is the same as the Speak It To Me command for increasing audio volume, so the volume got louder but the Save dialog did not come up. With the assistant's help, tester was able to access the File menu and was then able to independently navigate to the Save As option and use the Save As dialog box.

Task 5. Closing the file

Tester was able to use the Alt + Q keyboard command to save the file.

Task 6. Retrieving the file

The WordUp keyboard shortcut for bringing up the Open File is Alt + O, which is the same as the Speak It To Me command for setting user preferences. This caused Speak It To Me to abruptly shut down. We tried this two more times, and the same thing happened.

Task 7. Editing but not saving the file

No difficulties noted.

Task 8. Closing the application

Tester was able to use the Ctrl + Q keyboard command to start shutting down WordUp. Speak It To Me was not able to read the "Do you want to save your changes?" dialog, but it did read the "Yes/No/Cancel" buttons. The tester chose "No" and WordUp closed down successfully.

Try starting to address the issue by talking with technical support staff from the assistive technology manufacturer. They are more likely than the mainstream manufacturer to be able to analyze where the problem occurs, because they may have encountered similar problems in the past. They may also give you some questions to ask the mainstream manufacturer if the problem doesn't seem to be from the assistive side.

Sample Completed Assistive Technology Report Form #2

(*Note:* This sample is deliberately designed with minimal formatting to optimize compatibility with assistive technologies.)

Date: 5/8/2012
Tester: Barbara Gordon
Assistive Technology: Mr. Big magnification software
Application: Biblioworld library interface software

Task 1. Signing in

Biblioworld requires that the user sign in before accessing any applications. The instructions and text entry box were too small for the tester to see, and therefore she was not able to enter her library card number without assistance.

Task 2. Starting Mr. Big from the Biblioworld menu

The product icons were large enough for the tester to see without magnification, so she was able to start the program independently.

Task 3. Starting a word processing program from the Biblioworld menu

No problems noted.

Task 4. Returning to the interface software menu to select another program

The interface displayed an animated sequence before the tester returned to the menu. This could not be accessed using Mr. Big, and the tester complained that this was frustrating because she did not know whether the information presented in the sequence was important.

Task 5. Logging out

No problems noted.

When you are talking to any manufacturer, provide as much information as you can about the problem: when it happens (e.g., when the user begins typing), what happens, and whether the problem is consistently replicable. If possible, sit in front of the test computer when you are talking to representatives, because they may ask you to perform other tests and describe the results. If you or your testers have any suggestions on how the problems can be solved, provide these as well. For example, if administrative software requires users to sign in before they can select their assistive technology, suggest that this software provide large print and voice prompts just for the sign-in process.

Some mainstream manufacturers of library software may state that you're the only library to ever request accessibility modifications or may indicate that they feel these modifications would serve only a small audience. The Center for Accessible Technology has initiated efforts among a group of librarians, accessibility professionals, and American Library Association staff members to counteract these responses by making accessibility a purchasing requirement. If you'd like to be a part of this, please e-mail me at jane@janevincent.com. You may also want to develop library policies about acquisition of accessible software; a good example was created by the University of Wisconsin–Stevens Point library and is available at http://library.uwsp.edu/depts/colldev/disabil.htm.

If Applications Cannot Be Made Accessible

Where appropriate, the results of your testing procedure should be added to the forms you filled out for Chapter 3 and will ideally give you a clearer picture of what products to choose. But there will likely be times when, despite reasonable efforts, no assistive technology can be found that works with a given mainstream application. In this case, there are two primary solutions to consider:

1. For applications, see if an alternative can be made available. For example, if the library primarily offers access to word processing via an Internet-based program that proves inaccessible, see if the security setup can be modified on one or more computers so that assistive technology users can do word processing tasks on one of the simple programs built into the operating system.

2. For library software, provide clear information about known barriers and about contacting library staff for assistance. If, say, the login function is inaccessible, but the rest of the application works fine with assistive technology, then information about this can be provided via signage, as part of a training, or through other appropriate means.

Summary

A variety of factors may affect the ability of assistive technologies to work with the operating system, applications, specialized software, and files that your patrons will want to access. By understanding where incompatibilities are most likely to occur, keeping open lines of communication with IT staff, doing product testing as part of the assistive technology selection process, and following up as necessary with manufacturers, you will significantly increase the likelihood of purchasing products that will run smoothly on your library's computers. Of course, none of this effort will be meaningful if people with disabilities don't come to the library to use what you've installed. We'll look at marketing strategies in Chapter 5.

References

The Authors Guild. 2010. "White House Applauds Joint Effort for Print Disabled." The Authors Guild. http://www.authorsguild.org/advocacy/articles/white-house-applauds-joint-statement-on.html.

Barclay, Donald A. 2000. *Managing Public-Access Computers*. New York: Neal-Schuman.

Barnett, Andy. 2002. *Libraries, Community, and Technology*. Jefferson, NC: McFarland & Company.

Blansit, B. Douglas. 2011. "Common Computer Connectors and Important Characteristics." *Journal of Electronic Resources in Medical Libraries* 8, no. 1 (January–March): 87–98.

▶ **Companion Blog**

For resource updates, visit this book's companion blog at http://www.janevincent.com/iceact.

Blind Bargains (blog). 2011. "The Accessible Blio Reader." *Blind Bargains*, March 23. http://www.blindbargains.com/6thmode.php?m=6060.

El-Rahmin, Minara. 2010. "Kindle Lawsuit Settled by ASU and Blind Groups." *FindLaw* (blog), January 12. http://blogs.findlaw.com/injured/2010/01/kindle-lawsuit-settled-by-asu-and-blind-groups.html.

Nosowitz, Dan. 2009. "Amazon Caves to Snippy Authors: Kindle's Text-to-Voice Feature Now Optional." Gizmodo. February 28. http://i.gizmodo.com/5162143/amazon-caves-to-snippy-authors-kindles-text+to+voice-feature-now-optional.

Rothman, David H. 2006. "Razing the Tower of E-Babel." *Publishers Weekly* (blog), August 25. http://new.publishersweekly.com/pw/by-topic/columns-and-blogs/soapbox/article/8355-razing-the-tower-of-e-babel-.html.

Tatomir, Jennifer, and Joan C. Durrance. 2010. "Overcoming the Information Gap: Measuring the Accessibility of Library Databases to Adaptive Technology Users." *Library Hi-Tech* 28, no. 4: 577–594.

Tobias, Jim, and Jane Vincent. 2011. "Accessibility and E-readers." The Accessible Technology Coalition. http://atcoalition.org/article/accessibility-and-e-readers.

Usability One. 2009. "Accessibility Industry Report." Usability One. http://www.usabilityone.com/uploads/reports/UsabilityOne-Accessibility IndustryReport-Jan09.pdf.

Wikipedia. 2011. "Comparison of E-book Formats." Wikipedia. Accessed February 13. http://en.wikipedia.org/wiki/Comparison_of_e-book_formats.

Communicating with All Relevant Communities

A Market You Want

> It's one thing to hear people talk about a great program or service—it's an eye- and mind-opener to hear someone share about a love affair they're having with an organization and/or how they feel about belonging to a real community as a champion of their library. (Conley and Friedenwald-Fishman, 2009: 101)

Purchasing and installing assistive technology may be the first conscious step your library has taken toward serving patrons with disabilities. Sure, it's necessary for legislative compliance. But it's also an opportunity to initiate something that libraries already do well: identify an underserved group and take all appropriate steps to provide a holistic level of service. Part of that initiative should include a marketing strategy that lets your target audience members know you're now providing services with them in mind via communication channels they're comfortable with. Part of it includes preparing staff to provide these services at the highest possible level. And part of it involves knowing what services you won't be able to provide and where to refer people when appropriate.

Starting with Your Current Marketing Plan

> Allocating more resources to special groups targeted for outreach poses problems for some in the library profession. . . . When all services and programs are equally important, all are of the highest priority. All get an equal, albeit meager, share of the available resources. Marketing planning puts a different spin on equality. Market segmentation analysis gives you the tools to select a few markets on which to focus your efforts. Why? Because there are never enough resources to go around. Setting priorities is a must. (Fisher and Pride, 2006: 8)

Of all the sad words of tongue and pen, the saddest are these: "We put all this money, effort, and time into assistive computer technology, and no one uses it."

As we'll discuss in Chapter 6, using good outcome measurement may yield surprisingly positive usage information. Nevertheless, assuming that your goal is to approach equilibrium between availability and usage of assistive technology, it probably won't work to take the *Field of Dreams* approach and take for granted that if you install it, they will come. Because you've made a significant effort to attract people with disabilities to use your computers, why not think in terms of being poised to promote *all* the services of your library to a large and possibly untapped audience? To fully implement your assistive technology program, start with a simple credo: people with disabilities—using the broad definitions provided in Chapter 1—are a priority market for your library, and you want to attract and serve them.

In their book *Strategic Marketing for Non-Profit Organizations*, Kotler and Andreasen (2007) identify three core marketing strategies: *differentiation* (offering something not offered by competitors), *cost leadership* (offering something at the lowest cost), and *focus* (offering unique services to a specific, unserved market). Any or all of these may be important to targeting the market of people with disabilities and in setting priorities within that market.

- *Differentiation*. Title II of the Americans with Disabilities Act, which covers most libraries, says that your overall program needs to be accessible, but not every facility needs to have the same level of access (U.S. Department of Justice, 1993). If one of your library branches is located near a public computing site that provides accessible computers, then that branch may not need top prioritization in your own assistive technology efforts. However, if significant needs are identified that the nearby site isn't meeting—for example, they accommodate people with visual but not learning disabilities—then you may have identified a priority for your branch, which can be marketed accordingly.

- *Cost leadership*. Simply because library access is free doesn't automatically mean there aren't hidden costs for patrons. For many people with disabilities, these costs will include the effort and time necessary to get to and from your library. Is it easy to find information about your open hours? Is the primary branch where assistive technology will be housed near accessible public transit? Will there be good cell phone coverage when they need to call for a ride home?

- *Focus*. Many libraries have started their assistive technology services by focusing on blind users, only to be disappointed to find that most of this audience already has their own assistive technology set up at home. Your planning research and your selection process should have already provided information on at least one niche in your community where the actual need is greatest. This is probably the niche that you will also want to address first in your marketing.

Talk with patrons about unexpected factors that may affect their ability to get to your library. For example:

- Patrons who require attendant care may not be able to get to the library in the morning.
- Patrons who are dependent on public transit may be unwilling or unable to go to the library after dark.
- Patrons who rely on Social Security or other sources of fixed income may be able to afford to get to the library at the beginning of the month but not the end.

Using Appropriate Communication Channels

> To successfully serve the community we must try to see through our users' eyes. You may think that you are effectively communicating your message, but are you communicating in a way that your intended recipient can understand? Posters announcing a literacy program are not nearly as effective as announcements on the radio. Signs in English pointing the way to the foreign language collection send the wrong message. (Bremmer, 1994: 26)

Your library is probably already using a variety of communication channels for marketing: flyers, newsletter, website, local media, and so forth. Keep in mind that for people with disabilities, although you want the message to be the same as with other groups—"Visit and use your library; we have lots to offer you"—the accessibility of the medium itself will also send strong messages to your audience.

As part of surveying your community, you found out about what channels members use most often. Ideally, there was some overlap between these and the media you're already using to provide community outreach. Review the information about "Communication Methods and Accessibility Issues" in Chapter 1. Then think about the channels you want to use and the accessibility considerations associated with each.

> Something to consider for all your communication channels is casually including people with disabilities even where they're not the prime audience. For example, if you have a brochure page about your reference services, include a photo of an interaction where one of the participants has a visible disability.

Marketing Outside the Library: Getting the Message Across

> The marketing imagination is the starting point of success in marketing. It is distinguished from other forms of imagination by the unique insights it brings to understanding customers, their problems, and the means to capture their attention and their custom.... It is characterized by Leo McGinneva's famous clarification about why people buy quarter-inch drill bits: "They don't want quarter-inch bits. They want quarter-inch holes." (Levitt, 1986: 127–128)

From a marketing standpoint, your ultimate goal is to reach two reasonably distinct user groups of people with disabilities: those who know they want your computer services and those who don't. In this case, the latter population also splits into two groups, probably not as distinct: those who don't identify as having accessibility needs and those who don't identify as potential technology users.

For both groups, think about the "quarter-inch holes" your patrons may be seeking. Many modern libraries are seeking to reinvent themselves as community centers; will coming to the library to use assistive technology have the deeper effect of providing a social outlet? Can the library provide information not available elsewhere, or that users didn't know existed, both via computers and via other resources?

As you plan your marketing strategy, keep in mind that people with disabilities can be equally—or more—attracted to a lecture on caring for roses, or new books on playing the stock market, as they would be to presentations or materials specifically about disability. Your goal is to make all resources available in as equitable a format as possible, with an ongoing acknowledgment that accessible computers are an important, but not unique, part of realizing that goal.

Outreach to Self-Identified Users

> Don't become a "one-hit wonder," getting what you need and never coming back. Commit to the long term and take the initiative to follow up after completion of programs or initiatives to seek further collaboration and to understand where you can contribute to other priorities in the community. (Campisteguy and Friedenwald-Fishman, 2009: 11)

When you convened your focus groups, you probably identified at least some members of your prime audience: people who identify as both having a disability and as either current or want-to-be computer users. However, assistive technology alone may never be a sufficient reason for someone with a disability to come to your library.

One way to think about introducing assistive technology is that it's like washing a single dish after dinner. Have you ever done that and noticed that the faucet was streaky and could use a quick wipe down? And while you're thinking of it, it's probably a good time to set the oven to self-clean, and the shelf paper really could stand to be replaced. Before you know it, the process has snowballed and you find yourself with a really spiffed-up kitchen.

Introducing assistive technology is an opportunity to snowball your services to people with disabilities. Start by considering at least three areas: addressing unmet needs, collection development, and programming.

Addressing Unmet Needs

Review your focus group interactions for any concerns that people have beyond computer access. Do wheelchair users need an accessible meeting space? Are people who receive Social Security looking for a program about the potential impact on their benefits if they get married or start a new job? Are blind people interested in scheduling an orientation tour of the library that would help them navigate it independently on their next visit? Would community leaders like someone from the library to become a member of the local Independent Living Center board or sit on a transportation accessibility committee? As Maria Elena Campisteguy and Eric Friedenwald-Fishman (2009: 11) suggest, "Be supportive as issues important to the community come up, even if those issues are not always at the top of your own list of priorities. There is a critical role that individuals from outside a cultural group can play as effective and knowledgeable facilitators and advocates for change within a specific community."

Collection Development

If you don't have any disability-related materials, now is the perfect time to start. Ask focus group members and other contacts for suggestions.

The next time your library makes decisions on starting new magazine subscriptions, include a few targeted to people with disabilities—an excellent list is at http://www.netreach.net/~abrejcha/magazine.htm. Talk to your collection development colleagues about adding quality fiction, nonfiction, movies, and CDs related to disability. Don't forget the children's section; a good starting place is to look at the list of winners of the American Library Association's Schneider Family Book Awards, which "honor an author or illustrator for a book that embodies an artistic expression of the disability experience for child and adolescent audiences" (American Library Association, 2011). If you have a program encouraging everyone in your city or county to read the same book, think about titles that include positive portrayals of one or more people with disabilities as main or supporting characters, and always make sure that you can provide the book in alternative formats. All this can give people with disabilities more incentives to come in to the library and shows that you're thinking holistically about your audience.

Programming

Programming, like marketing, requires two considerations. One is providing some programs that will be attractive specifically to people with disabilities; the other is making sure that any program will be accessible. The bibliography lists several sources of practical information to help with the latter consideration. As for the former, while input on topics from patrons is always useful, there are also ways to be proactive. Introducing your assistive technology is a logical topic for a program. Other presentations might focus on legislative changes, new municipal construction that may provide access benefits or barriers, or speakers from local groups that have a disability focus. Make sure to include your contacts in the disability community when advertising any program likely to be of interest to a broad range of groups, such as a "meet the mayoral candidates" event. Ask attendees to fill out a form with their contact information so that you can include them in your evaluation process (see Chapter 6). The form should include a way for them to indicate any format preference for participating in surveys, interviews, and so forth.

Outreach to Other Potential Users

Eileen Elliott de Saez (2002) identifies five stages within a user adoption process: Awareness (the user knows that a service exists but not what it offers or how to take advantage of it), Interest (the user discovers a stimulus to seek more information), Risk Appraisal (the user considers the benefits and disadvantages of trying the service), Experimentation (the user tries out the service if it is offered on a trial basis and won't take too much time, effort, or expense), and Adoption (the user makes regular and full use of the service).

Progress through most of these stages is entirely dependent on the user's motivation and actions. The area where you are most likely to have an impact is Interest, where the user finds a reason to bridge the

> ▶ **Companion Blog**

Information about notable new books or other materials on disability will be tracked in this book's companion blog at http://www.janevincent.com/iceact.

Making materials of interest easy to find can be a draw, too. The Oakland (CA) Public Library developed a series of pictograms representing the most commonly requested Dewey categories and mounted them on their bookshelves. These have proven to be a useful strategy for helping people find the nonfiction they want without having to read or understand Dewey numbers; positive response has come from individuals with learning disabilities as well as parents pleased that their young children can find the dinosaur section without assistance. The pictograms can be downloaded from http://libraryliteracy.org/staff/differences/dewey.html and used free of charge.

Librarians at the Antioch (CA) Public Library noted that a group of adults with cognitive disabilities regularly visited the library but did not engage with any of the library's services. In response, library staff developed the Wednesday Club, with a range of programming including computer classes, presentations about local wildlife, and yoga instruction. The library won an ASCLA award in 2008 for this program and has provided a video and a manual on how to reproduce the program in other libraries at http://guides.ccclib.org/insiders.

gap between awareness of a service and at least consideration of adopting it. The more reasons any given user finds, the more likely he or she will be to find a stimulus that fits his or her priorities and subsequently move to additional stages of the adoption process.

One way to address increasing interest levels is to consider Pip Coburn's Change Function, which states that: "If the level of crisis is higher than the total perceived pain of adopting a new solution, then a change will occur. If the crisis is lower than the total perceived pain of adoption, then things will stay as they are" (Coburn, 2006: 28). What might "crisis" and "pain" mean to people with disabilities, whether or not they identify as such, in regards to learning about your assistive technology services and deciding whether to use them?

A likely high-level crisis for people who don't have computer access elsewhere involves needing to use the ever-increasing number of services that are available only online, whether these involve applying for jobs, cutting through governmental red tape, or communicating with banks and other companies. Lower level, but still influential, crises might involve finding materials relevant to hobbies and interests or staying in touch with friends or family members who communicate only via e-mail. For people who already use library computers, the crisis might involve dissatisfaction with the existing setup coupled with a lack of any exposure to assistive technology options. All of these are situations where use of accessible computers in the library can address a community need.

In the following two sections, we'll look at what the pain of adopting a new solution might mean to potential assistive technology users and how to address this pain in ways that help patrons move through the Interest stage toward becoming experimenters and, ideally, adopters.

Getting Past Access Reluctance

> People on the receiving end of our beneficence *do* have reactions of reluctance, resistance, and rejection. Are they all dysfunctional fools, or are they just paying resentful attention to the social markers invisibly embossed on every manufactured object? If an upscale watch means "I'm stylish and rich," what does a reacher mean? And what does giving someone a reacher mean? (Tobias, 2009)

Several buses in Berkeley have a row of three seats at the front specifically designated for priority seating, next to a lower, single seat. I was riding home one afternoon when a woman at least 70 years old, moving slowly using a walker, boarded and snapped at a 40ish man sitting in the single seat to yield it. Startled, the man complied, but politely pointed out that there were three priority seats available.

"Oh no," the woman declaimed. "THOSE are for seniors and disabled!"

How do you market a service to members of a group who don't identify with the group or who may even have a vested interest in not identifying to avoid feeling stigmatized? For people with "access reluctance," pain (to cite Cobern's function) might mean having to acknowledge that unadapted computers simply don't work for them because their physical or cognitive realities don't allow them to access the monitor, keyboard, mouse, or information effectively.

Fortunately, marketers have come up with ways to bypass the need to experience this pain before making a change. Two strategies appear frequently for marketing mainstream products that address accessibility in some way, and both are likely to be useful to libraries:

- *Hide the pain.* Whole ad campaigns are built around convincing people to use a product because of the limitations of competing products. One of the most successful was the Gap's line of "easy-fit" jeans. Their real purpose was to accommodate middle-aged spread, but no one wants to be reminded that they're putting on weight. "Easy-fit" puts the emphasis where it should be: on the appropriateness of the jeans, not the weight of the wearer. Other examples are nonprescription hearing aids that are marketed as a way to get "super hearing" to spy on your neighbors and pocket magnifiers that focus on the problem of tiny print on menus, not the issue of declining boomer visual acuity.

  Sometimes this attitude is built into the product design itself via a sort of euphemistic approach: it looks like something other than what it is. Contemporary hearing aids, for example, may look like MP3 players or Bluetooth headsets; they're not hidden, but they're not conspicuous.

  Some potential assistive technology users may need extra convincing. How do you address these users without confusing others who may be specifically looking for "disability services"? One way to do this is via carefully worded signage and other collateral. If you were only thinking in terms of addressing legal obligations, these might say something like, "Ask us about assistive technology to help people with disabilities." However, to maximize your audience, try putting the emphasis on the failures of the standard computer: "Computer print too small? Mouse driving you crazy? Ask us about alternative technologies and strategies."

- *Share the pain.* Celebrity endorsement is an all-round effective advertising strategy, and it's no different for accessibility. In 2006, the makers of the pain medication Aleve ran a Super Bowl ad showing *Star Trek's* Leonard Nimoy having trouble making his trademark Vulcan hand signal, until a magic dose of Aleve lets him get up in front of a convention and do his thing. There's no public evidence outside of this commercial that Nimoy has arthritis or any other significant dexterity issues, but that may be irrelevant. Take Aleve, says the message, and be able to do difficult hand movements just like Spock.

  Within a local community of people with disabilities, "celebrity" may translate into identity as either an official or de facto leader. Try to identify these individuals and court them. (The members of your focus group are probably good people to start with.) For example, offer to provide a special opportunity for them to get an assistive technology demonstration. If

This approach to hearing aids is actually nothing new. Since the 1800s, they've been hidden in hats, fans, purses, and broaches (Washington University School of Medicine, 2009).

they like what they see, they can be powerful ambassadors. You might also want to invite other prominent local individuals, such as the mayor or the head of an important local business, and try to get some press about their visit.

Getting Past Computer Reluctance

To revisit an analogy cited earlier, computers are now and have always been drill bits rather than holes. Users have to want to *do* something using a computer to have a successful experience. If users don't have a particular agenda—or worse, if they've been scared by beliefs such as "computers are only about pornography and viruses"—they will be unlikely to see any reason at all to come to your library and use your computers. Another reason users may have for "computer reluctance" might be that they actually do want to use computers but assume that because of their disability they either won't be able to use one or won't be able to use the ones at the library.

This is where good programming can be helpful. Set up a presentation about finding information on topics likely to be of interest to your target community—for example, for elders, this could include health, genealogy, tracking stocks, or volunteer opportunities. Use the computer as one type of information resource they can use. Discretely slip in accommodation information—"My, the print on that website is small. Let me use the browser settings options to make it more legible." Once your potential audience has a feel for how computers might be relevant to them, and an awareness that their disability won't shut them out of computer use, they will start to develop more reasons to explore. One of these may be the stimulus necessary for them to move into the Risk Appraisal stage of adoption and ideally beyond.

The "share the pain" strategy mentioned earlier may also work. If a group leader gets enthused about what computers can do and starts showing off his or her new knowledge to other group members, it can be contagious.

Outreach to Agents

Sometimes the most appropriate way to reach your target audience can be through an agent, who will then pass information along. Agents could be almost anyone: parents or children of people with disabilities, professionals such as teachers and doctors, friends, colleagues, and so on.

The best way to do this is to provide information about your accessibility services where everyone can become aware of it. Put brochures about your assistive technology in your main information area. Have a prominent link to disability/elder services on your website. If you have a regular podcast, do a segment on your new assistive technologies.

This is another place where holistic thinking about communication channels becomes useful. If all your brochures are in large print, people whose parents are starting to experience vision loss won't think twice about picking them up and passing them on. If there is information provided on your program announcements that real-time captioning is available on request, audiologists will be able to encourage patients with newly diagnosed hearing loss that the library is one public place that can accommodate them.

Marketing Inside the Library: Preparing Your Staff

> The most valuable piece of equipment in a library to assist consumers with disabilities . . . is not equipment at all. It is a friendly, knowledgeable librarian. (Coombs, 2000: 285)

> In the final analysis stereotypes and prejudice are overcome by contact with *real* persons who are disabled. If library staff members continue to promote isolation by excluding persons with disabilities from library activities, the stereotypes and prejudices are likely to persist. (Wright and Davie, 1991: 114–115)

Funny thing about a successful marketing campaign: you invite people to show up, and they show up. If staff members aren't prepared, they will quickly get overwhelmed. When the people who show up represent a population that the library has not proactively served in the past, such as people with disabilities, staff discomfort may be even more profound. They may have no sense of practical strategies for communicating with these new patrons, let alone an awareness of etiquette. They may also be embarrassed by a lack of knowledge about specific services, such as assistive technology, that people are asking about. A thoughtful training program will help prepare staff members to turn curious first-time visitors into loyal patrons.

TRAINING IN ACTION

Ann Arbor District Library

Professor Jack Bernard is, among other distinctions, the chair of the University of Michigan's Council on Disability Concerns. When he took me on a tour of the Ann Arbor (MI) District Library, which had recently incorporated the Washtenaw County Library for the Blind and Physically Disabled, I wasn't expecting him to walk up to several staff members and casually ask them about the library's disability services. But I was pleased to find that everyone we talked to provided helpful, accurate, and respectful responses.

I asked Terry Soave, the library's Outreach & Neighborhood Services Manager, for information on the training they had used to achieve such positive results, and she provided the following.

Following a brief three-month transition period when patrons formerly served by the Washtenaw County Library for the Blind and Physically Disabled were served through the Services for the Blind & Physically Handicapped Regional Library (SBPH) in Lansing, Michigan, in January 2009, the Ann Arbor District Library (AADL) began administering the Washtenaw Library for the Blind and Physically Disabled (WLBPD@AADL), opening for service February 2, 2009. In preparation for taking on this new service, administration and management staff at AADL met with the former County library administration and staff and also with staff from the SBPH. It was during that period that a variety of information was exchanged and training opportunities began taking shape.

While several core staff training components have been established, WLBPD@AADL training continues to be developed and is facilitated in an on-going, as well as an as-needed basis, and is provided through a variety of means.

(Continued)

TRAINING IN ACTION *(Continued)*

As is our goal in providing patron access to all services at AADL, it is also our goal that anybody seeking the services of the WLBPD@AADL shall be accommodated at any of our five locations in-person, by phone, or by e-mail; and in a timely, professional, and customer-service–centered manner.

Training provided to all public services staff prior to the transition:
Public services staff refers to approximately 175 full and part-time staff representing the following departments: Circulation, Access & User Services (AUS), Outreach & Neighborhood Services (ONS), Youth Services, and some Information Technology (IT) and Security staff.

SBPH staff provided site visits during which AADL staff received the following:
- Background on the history and structure of National Library Service for the Blind and Physically Handicapped Network Library Services (NLS)
- Training on how to use the Consortium of User Libraries (CUL) software system for registration, selection, circulation, and inventory control for materials circulated to WLBPD@AADL patrons
- Training on how to assist blind and physically disabled persons both practically and sensitively

IT and Circulation staff also met with IT staff from the SBPH and the developers of CUL to determine the best method for networking CUL to make it available to all staff using AADL computers at all five AADL locations.

Orientation training for ALL new hires system-wide, provided up to twice-monthly:
- Information on what it means that AADL serves as the WLBPD, what to expect, and what is expected of them
- Training on how to assist blind and physically disabled persons both practically and sensitively

These trainings are facilitated by the manager and staff from the ONS department.

Quarterly two-hour trainings for all newly hired public services staff (also offered to regular staff as a refresher and/or as one-on-one training by request):
- Background on the history and structure of NLS
- Training on how to use the CUL software system for registration, selection, circulation, and inventory control for materials circulated to WLBPD@AADL patrons
- Training on what resources are available to staff to assist them with assisting patrons and where each resource may be located
- A tour and introduction to the Assistive Technology Lab, the services offered, and training on the level of support expected of staff upon patron request.

These trainings are facilitated by the manager and staff from the ONS department.

New-hire materials processing training:
All new Circulation materials processors are trained either one-on-one, or if more than one is hired at a given time, together, on materials processing procedures by a Circulation Supervisor.

Readily accessible staff resources:
There are always some staff members who are more familiar with and/or excel at providing certain aspects of the service than others. We encourage staff to both rely on and assist each other whenever possible. This is done in all of the following ways:
- Side-by-side at a public service desk
- Behind the scenes while following up on a patron request or processing materials
- By calling another staff member on the phone
- By e-mailing the wlbpd@aadl.org e-mail address, which goes to several staff members' inboxes directly and is checked regularly for follow up
- By accessing any staff member system-wide who may have an answer to a question through "The Channel," a staff-only online chat room

(Continued)

Another readily available staff resource is the WLBPD@AADL portal on the staff wiki. This is a designated area on the staff wiki that addresses all things WLBPD-related in detail, from all the things covered in in-person trainings; to statistics; to how to navigate through CUL to order materials or update a patron account; to how to request a title currently not available be recorded by the SBPH; to how to assist patrons with applying for and downloading books from BARD; to helpful NLS resources—and much, much more!

As is the nature of any wiki, it's a dynamic—or "living"—documentation for staff to reference and also update as needed. Responsibility for making sure the information on the wiki is accurate and up-to-date is that of all staff, whether they are actually making the updates themselves or notifying a more appropriate person that an update is needed.

E-mail updates:

Managers and staff are easily able to send out updates to staff to draw their attention to changes made to the wiki or to announce a newly added service; promote a training opportunity; or to otherwise inform staff by selecting the appropriate group e-mail to send the information to. All staff are required to check their e-mail on a regular basis to remain current with organizational information of all sorts.

(*Source*: Terry Soave, e-mail communication, October 12, 2010. Provided courtesy of the Ann Arbor District Library.)

The following information isn't intended to substitute for a training program. Rather, it's intended as an overview of the topics that should be covered, either by library staff or outside consultants, as part of any training that's offered to get staff prepared for a rollout of assistive technology services.

Using Appropriate Language

There are several guides to appropriate language when referring to people with various types of disabilities. One that's been around for a long time is *Guidelines for Reporting and Writing about People with Disabilities* from the University of Kansas (available online at http://www.rtcil.org/products/RTCIL%20publications/Media/Guidelines%20for%20Reporting%20and%20Writing%20about%20People%20with%20Disabilities%207th%20Edition.pdf). The Guidelines reflect the current movement toward "people-first" language—mentioning the person and then the disability, as in, "woman with Down syndrome," "doctor who is hard of hearing," and so forth. Other resources are listed in the bibliography.

While these guidelines are a good starting point, especially for written materials, it's important to realize that there isn't a consensus among people with disabilities themselves. Some blind people, for example, have been outspoken opponents of people-first language (Vaughn, 2009). People who have never had hearing may refer to themselves as being Deaf (part of a cultural and linguistic minority) rather than as deaf (having a medical condition) and not identify with having a disability at all (Padden, 1989); this is why you will see references such as "Deaf and disabled services." Some people with mobility impairments may use the words "cripple" or "crip" in the same way other groups use taboo words—acceptable and even empowering within a group, offensive

There *is* general agreement about avoiding cutesy or tragic language. Phrases like "physically challenged," "differently abled," and "handi-capable" were probably generated by nondisabled people and have been extensively parodied, never better than by writer Pamela Walker (2005: 6), who says, "I like to think of us as Severely Labeled." Descriptions of people with disabilities as being a "victim of..." or "suffering from..." carry an undesirable and unnecessary tone of pity. An accurate but emotionally neutral alternative was used in a 2010 *Los Angeles Times* obituary for a famous advocate and author whose disability was described simply by saying "[he] came down with polio" (Nelson, 2010).

Several libraries have adopted the term "ADA patron." This could be appropriate if you are truly using the Americans with Disabilities Act definitions to determine who can and can't use your assistive technology. Realize, however, that this will leave out many people with mild to moderate disabilities, including most elders, people with repetitive strain injuries in only one hand, people with short-term disabilities, and so forth.

when used by outsiders—while others may find them inappropriate in any situation; Laura Hershey provides a wonderful essay about this at http://www.cripcommentary.com/cc090299.html. Mary Johnson, former editor of the *Disability Rag* magazine (now called *Ragged Edge*), sums up the reasons for these discrepancies: "[T]he disability rights movement is no different from any other group.... Although each term has its supporters who come up with rationales for the term's being the 'best' one, the real truth is that it has to do with politics and power within the minority. That is why the issue of whether a term is 'negative' is really not germane to which word will define a group" (Johnson, 1994: 28).

The best strategy is to talk with your focus groups to find out what terms are locally preferred among people with particular types of disabilities, taking into account that these preferences may also vary among different age and ethnic groups. However, an overall attitude that treats people with disabilities as being as valuable as any other patrons will ultimately trump linguistics. As Darlys Vander Beek, a former Disabled Student Services director at the University of Michigan, used to wryly joke: "What do you call a person with a disability? Fred...."

The same strategy also applies to other cohorts within your broader definition of disability. For example, a 2007 survey of the Journalists Exchange on Aging found that "senior" is acceptable terminology for describing people over 65, "elderly" is demeaning while "elder" conveys respect, and "boomer" is fine as long as the "baby" is dropped (Gardner, 2007). Check with your elder contacts to verify that they agree with these conventions.

Etiquette

Rhea Rubin has written a superb series of guides for libraries on the practical aspects of communicating with disabled people in library settings; a summary of her tips is included at the end of this chapter (pp. 96–97). Other guidelines intended to ensure courteous interactions with people with various types of disabilities are listed in the bibliography. In my experience, these boil down to four basic principles, with the acronym ROAR:

1. *Respect the individual.* Ninety-nine people with learning disabilities may have requested one type of accommodation, but the 100th might want something different. If possible, provide that different accommodation. As Robert Begg (1982: 19) writes, "The staff must remember that each disabled patron is an individual with his own character, problems, needs, and ambitions. A reasonable approach to library service for the handicapped therefore requires a balancing of sensitivity, common sense and respect."

2. *Offer assistance, not insistence.* A person with Down syndrome who seems at first glance to be lost may actually know her way around the library perfectly well but be temporarily distracted. On the other hand, a tall man who in theory should have no

problems selecting a book from the top shelf might have low vision or a painfully sprained shoulder. Use the same judgment skills you'd use in deciding whether any patron needs an offer of assistance, and take "no" for an answer.

As a corollary: unless there is an immediate risk of serious danger, never grab and steer a patron without asking permission first. Besides demonstrating courtesy, this may well be for your own protection. You never know when a blind patron might also have a black belt in Aikido and instinctively react by delivering an elegant but painful self-defense move.

3. *Apply the "Jordan test."* Take what you already know about other courteous interactions and think about how they might apply to disabled people. Would you approach someone wearing a beautiful sari and start fondling it? Then apply the same restraint to touching someone's wheelchair. (Would you act differently if the sari or the wheelchair were on fire? Of course.) After an introduction to a lesbian couple, would your first question be about their sex life? Then consider the parallel to starting a conversation with a head injury survivor by asking, "So, what happened to you?" Would you provide unsolicited information about skin-altering cosmetics to a person of color? Then avoid creating the situation that David Roche, who speaks all over the country about his facial disfigurement, encountered in a hospital library: "One of the librarians came up to me as I was bent over my books. She said, 'I thought you might be interested in this,' and set in front of me a booklet entitled *The Let's Face It Resource Guide for People with Facial Difference*. She quickly walked away. I was angry and embarrassed. I brought the booklet home and showed it to Marlena. I told her, 'I want nothing to do with this'" (Roche, 2008: 110).

4. *Relax.* People are people. There will be some patrons with disabilities—and some without—who will take umbrage no matter what you do or say. The majority, however, will be appreciative of sincere efforts and respond in kind.

Part of relaxing is avoiding self-consciousness. A good example of this is a natural use of language. We use a lot of idioms tied to standard physical capabilities—"See you later," "Did you hear about...?," "It's just a short walk," and so on. Go ahead and use these same idioms even when communicating with people who can't literally see, hear, or walk. It conveys that you're comfortable with the interaction. Another example is offering to shake hands, even if the person is wearing a prosthetic or seems to have poor hand strength. This is a situation that people will have almost inevitably encountered before, and they will generally use body language to show you if they prefer a modification, such as shaking with their left hand.

Yes, you'll make an occasional faux pas. So does everyone. I once observed a blind colleague of mine approach another member of a panel discussion that had just ended. He said, "I

I named the Jordan test after I. King Jordan, the first Deaf president of Gaulladet, the first university for the Deaf in the United States. After being repeatedly asked during a *60 Minutes* interview if he wanted his hearing back, his friendly demeanor finally cracked and he shot back, "That's almost like asking a black person if he would rather be white" (Lane, 2005).

An etiquette-related topic that has been of particular concern to libraries involves service animals. As of this writing, the Americans with Disabilities Act regulations have been modified so that, in most cases, only dogs can be classified as service animals (some exceptions can be made for well-behaved miniature horses), and then only if they have been trained to perform a specific task—for example, a dog that has been trained to recognize its owner's signs of depression and respond by licking his hand is a service animal, but a dog that simply makes the owner feel more secure by its presence is not. A good summary of the new regulations is available at http://www.mhtl.com/assets/PDF/NEW-ADA-Regulations-Regarding-the-Presence-and-Use-of-Service-Animals-February-2011.pdf.

don't believe we've met," and extended his hand. Casually, she replied, "I know we haven't; if we had, you'd know I have no arms." With a chuckle, he put his hand down, and they immediately began a congenial conversation.

Staff Training on Assistive Technology

Librarians do have a distinct advantage over anyone else when it comes to any technology training: we think like librarians. That is, we don't necessarily memorize information so much as we memorize how and where to find information. In your current technology trainings, this might translate into informing staff that they need to know what applications do and where to find a list of commands but not into memorizing all the commands for a given application.

The same strategy works for assistive technology. For example, cheat sheets are useful for prompting staff on basic commands, encouraging them to try using the software on their own, and reminding them about where to get more information. These can also be distributed in various formats to users, or laminated and attached to the CPU where they're loaded. (A sample cheat sheet is available below.)

Think about how assistive technology training will fit into your current training plan. Make sure that each session involves a presentation from someone well versed in both how and when each specific product should be used—ideally, someone who uses the product themselves. Use

Sample Cheat Sheet for Assistive Technology Software

Read Me First!

Read Me First! is software that will read text on the computer screen. First use the Highlight tool to select the text; then click on the Play button to hear the text. A Voice Options tool lets you choose whether a male or a female voice is used and how fast text is read.

The Read Me First! interface looks like this:

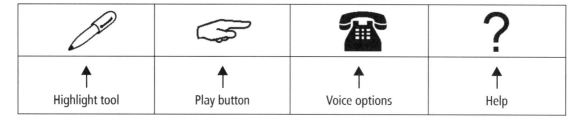

| Highlight tool | Play button | Voice options | Help |

A Read Me First! manual can be requested from the Reference Desk.

For more information about the product, including how to get a demonstration version to try on your computer at home, contact:

Vapor Software
1000 Cemetery Lane
Winterwood, CA 99999
(415) 555-0001
http://www.havingvapors.com/

the same policies as for other trainings; if new hires are expected to go through your training sessions for other applications, then they should also attend sessions on assistive technology basics. If you designate one or more staff members as the library expert on other applications, make sure that some are designated as assistive technology experts, give them practice time and/or extended training on the applications in question, and have a back-up plan for times when no expert is available.

Providing Referrals to External Resources

As much as they might like to, librarians simply are not in a position to answer all questions and provide all services related to assistive technology. This includes issues such as providing extended training on technology use, identifying the most effective technology for their needs, or addressing the requirements of people who can't be served by what the library provides.

The Americans with Disabilities Act of 1990 requires only "reasonable modifications" that would not "fundamentally alter the nature of its service, program, or activity" or "result in an undue burden" (Americans with Disabilities Act, 1991). Providing extensive one-on-one training on any application, or purchasing any and all equipment that users request, would probably be a fundamental alteration whether it involves assistive or mainstream technology. Therefore, your focus will sometimes be on providing appropriate referrals.

To supplement the community resources that you found while doing assistive technology planning (see Chapter 1), the following are some nationwide resources where you can refer individuals for direct assistance or additional information:

Consider developing a handout of referrals not only to resources related to assistive technology but also to other community resources of likely interest to people with disabilities, such as the nearest Independent Living Center, the local Department of Rehabilitation office, and so on.

- Every state and territory has a federally funded Assistive Technology Act center. These centers have information on finding recycled equipment, funding resources, and referrals to other relevant organizations within the state. They also sponsor programs that loan some types of equipment on a short-term basis. A list of all AT Act centers is at http://www.ataporg.org/atap/index?id=states_listing.

- The Alliance for Technology Access (ATA) has demonstration centers in 24 states and the Virgin Islands. These centers have a variety of assistive computer technologies on display and are able to provide information and demonstrations, usually for free or at low cost. A list of ATA centers is at http://www.ataccess.org/index.php?option=com_content&view=article&id=16&Itemid=22.

- Microsoft has several Accessibility Resource Centers across the United States; a list of these is at http://www.microsoft.com/enable/centers/marc.aspx. Microsoft also maintains a list of other national and international resources at http://www.microsoft.com/enable/centers/worldwide.aspx.

Checklist: Tips for Serving People with Disabilities

General Service Guidelines

❑ Be aware that visiting the library may be one of a limited number of social contact opportunities for some patrons with disabilities. Make an extra, but not exaggerated, effort to be welcoming and helpful.

❑ Treat the person with respect and without condescension.

❑ Assume that the interests and needs of people with disabilities are as wide ranging as those of the general population. Don't assume that their primary purpose for visiting relates to their disability.

❑ Don't assume that a patron with disabilities needs extra assistance or different treatment.

❑ Act naturally. For example, offer to shake hands with a person who is wearing a prosthetic hand.

❑ Don't touch the person or their equipment, service dog, etc. without permission.

❑ If a companion or device is used to facilitate communication, look at and speak to the patron, not the companion or device, as much as possible.

❑ Ask what communication method, materials format, etc. the patron prefers.

❑ Be patient. Don't finish a patron's sentences for them.

❑ If users seem to be having difficulty with tasks such as filling out forms or using self-checkout kiosks, offer assistance whether or not they are obviously disabled.

❑ Keep major pathways unobstructed.

❑ Initially assume that unusual behavior relates to a disability, not inebriation.

Serving Patrons Who Are Deaf or Hard of Hearing

❑ Approach users so that you can be seen.

❑ Get users' attention before you start speaking.

❑ Don't assume knowledge of sign language or lipreading.

❑ Don't leave to find a person who can sign unless the patron requests it.

❑ Reduce background noise or move to a quieter location.

❑ Always face users as you speak and maintain eye contact.

❑ Speak at a normal pace, enunciating carefully; do not exaggerate your lip movements or mumble as this makes speech reading difficult.

❑ Keep your mouth visible; do not obscure it with your hands or by chewing. If you have a moustache, be aware that this may complicate lipreading.

❑ Be aware of the lighting. Don't stand in front of a light source, as that makes it difficult to speech read or pick up visual cues.

❑ If patrons have hearing aids or other assistive listening devices, give them an opportunity to adjust the equipment.

❑ If patrons do not seem to understand you, write it down.

Serving Patrons Who Are Blind or Visually Impaired

❑ Do not yell or speak loudly.

❑ Identify yourself and others with you. If in a group setting, remember to identify the person you are addressing. If you need to leave, let the patron know.

❑ When giving directions, use a clock face as your basis. For example, "The reference desk is at three o'clock from where you're facing."

❑ When guiding patrons, stand next to them and slightly ahead, then offer to let them take your arm or elbow.

❑ Do not leave patrons standing without letting them know you're leaving and whether you'll be back.

(Continued)

Checklist: Tips for Serving People with Disabilities *(Continued)*

Serving Patrons with Learning Disabilities

❏ Give clear directions, checking for comprehension, and paraphrasing or repeating as necessary.

❏ Recognize that patrons may need extra time to understand you or to complete a task.

❏ Be literal. Some patrons may have difficulty with tonal subtleties and with metaphors.

❏ Offer information in a variety of reading and comprehension levels and in nonprint formats.

Serving Patrons with Cognitive Disabilities

❏ Be literal. Some patrons may have difficulty with tonal subtleties and metaphors.

❏ Provide materials that are age-appropriate but at a lower reading level.

❏ Use clear and simple language when giving directions or assistance. Repeat if you feel that the person has not understood.

❏ Allow extra time to understand instructions.

❏ If possible, use demonstrations instead of verbal instructions.

❏ Do not be offended if a person does not respond to you. Again, allow extra time.

❏ Some people may not be able to control their behavior. As long as their actions are not disturbing or frightening to other users or staff, be tolerant and flexible.

❏ Because reading can be difficult, emphasize books with photographs and illustrations, and multi-media materials. Multi-sensory materials (such as captioned videos) are especially good.

Serving Patrons with Mental or Emotional Disabilities

❏ Recognize that some patrons may feel uncomfortable making eye contact and respect this.

❏ Many patrons may feel the general population fears and avoids them and thus appreciate all respectful and friendly interactions. However, people with some types of mental illness, such as severe depression or schizophrenia, may be shy of social interaction. Be friendly but do not persist if the person does not respond.

❏ Do not take a patron's behavior personally. For example, a person with Tourette's syndrome may blurt out obscenities but these are not directed at anyone in particular.

❏ If a patron behaves strangely but is not disturbing others (e.g., a schizophrenic talking quietly to an invisible companion), ignore it. Unless absolutely necessary, do not try to correct the person's perception or impose your sense of reality.

❏ Most patrons are not threatening. If, however, someone shows threatening behavior, standard library policy for such situations should be followed.

Serving Patrons with Ambulatory Disabilities or Short Stature

❏ Ask the patron if they would like you to place yourself at their eye level by sitting or kneeling.

❏ Offer assistance to retrieve books or other objects that may be out of reach.

Serving Patrons with Speech Disabilities

❏ If you are unsure what the person is saying, repeat it back, asking for confirmation that you have understood.

❏ Try asking yes-and-no questions that the person can easily answer.

❏ If you still cannot understand, tell them and ask how you can communicate more easily.

❏ Offer writing as an alternative means of communication. Note that some causes of speech difficulty also make writing arduous.

❏ Consider moving to a quiet, less public area. Stress may exacerbate speech difficulties.

(Thanks to Jen McDonald-Peltier for her input. Source: Reprinted by permission of the author, Rhea Joyce Rubin. http://www.rheajoycerubin.org/.)

► **Companion Blog**

For resource updates, visit this book's companion blog at http://www.janevincent.com/iceact.

Summary

Once your assistive technology is in place, you'll need to advertise it and know how best to welcome the people who come to the library to use it. With appropriate staff training, you'll be prepared for your assistive technology efforts to succeed—and Chapter 6 will give you ways to measure that success.

References

American Library Association. 2011. "The Schneider Family Book Award." American Library Association. http://www.ala.org/ala/awardsgrants/awardsrecords/schneideraward/schneiderfamily.cfm.

Americans with Disabilities Act of 1990. 1991. Public L. No. 101-336, 104 Stat., § 35.104 {1991}.

Begg, Robert T. 1982. "Disabled Libraries: An Examination of Physical and Attitudinal Barriers to Handicapped Library Users." In *The Mainstreamed Library: Issues, Ideas, Innovations*, edited by Barbara H. Baskin and Karen H. Harris, 11–23. Chicago: American Library Association.

Bremmer, Suzanne W. 1994. *Long Range Planning: A How-To-Do-It Manual for Public Libraries*. New York: Neal-Schuman.

Campisteguy, Maria Elena, and Eric Friedenwald-Fishman. 2009. "Increasing Relevance, Relationships, and Results: Principles and Practices for Effective Multicultural Communication." In *The Library PR Handbook: High-Impact Communications*, edited by Mark R. Gould, 1–22. Chicago: American Library Association.

Coburn, Pip. 2006. *The Change Function*. New York: Portfolio.

Conley, Chip, and Eric Friedenwald-Fishman. 2009. "Building a Community: Empowering People as Messengers." In *The Library PR Handbook: High-Impact Communications*, edited by Mark R. Gould, 95–101. Chicago: American Library Association.

Coombs, Norman. 2000. "More than Technology." *Library Hi Tech News* 18, no. 3: 285–288.

Elliott de Saez, Eileen. 2002. *Marketing Concepts for Libraries and Information Services*. London: Facet Publishing.

Fisher, Patricia H., and Marseille M. Pride. 2006. *Blueprint for Your Library Marketing Plan: A Guide to Help You Survive and Thrive*. Chicago: American Library Association.

Gardner, Marilyn. 2007. "The Names We Use for People Over 50." *The Christian Science Monitor*, August 8. http://www.csmonitor.com/2007/0808/p15s01-lign.html.

Johnson, Mary. 1994. "Sticks and Stones: The Language of Disability." In *The Disabled, the Media, and the Information Age*, edited by Jack A. Nelson, 25–43. Westport, CT: Greenwood Press.

Kotler, Philip, and Alan R. Andreasen 2007. *Strategic Marketing for Non-Profit Organizations*. 7th ed. Upper Saddle River, NJ: Prentice Hall.

Lane, Harlan. 2005. "Ethnicity, Ethics, and the Deaf-World." *Journal of Deaf Studies and Deaf Education* 10, no. 3: 291–310. http://jdsde.oxfordjournals.org/content/10/3/291.full.

Levitt, Theodore. 1986. *The Marketing Imagination*. New York: The Free Press.

Nelson, Valerie J. 2010. "Paul K. Longmore Dies at 64; Leading Disability Scholar and Activist." *Los Angeles Times*, August 15. http://articles.latimes.com/2010/aug/15/local/la-me-paul-longmore-20100816.

Padden, Carol. 1989. "The Deaf Community and the Culture of Deaf People." In *American Deaf Culture*, edited by Sherman Wilcox, 1–16. Silver Spring, MD: Linstok Press.

Roche, David. 2008. *The Church of 80% Sincerity*. New York: Perigee.

Tobias, Jim. 2009. "Do Not Go Gentle into That Good Grip." *Inclusive Technologies* (blog), April 26. http://inclusive.com/2009/04/do-not-go-gentle-into-that-good-grip.

U.S. Department of Justice. 1993. *The Americans with Disabilities Act: Title II Technical Assistance Manual*. U.S. Department of Justice. http://www.ada.gov/taman2.html.

Vaughn, C. Edwin. 2009. "People-First Language: An Unholy Crusade." *Braille Monitor*, March. http://www.nfb.org/images/nfb/Publications/bm/bm09/bm0903/bm090309.htm.

Walker, Pamela Kay. 2005. *Moving Over the Edge: Artists with Disabilities Take the Leap*. Davis, CA: Michael Horton Media.

Washington University School of Medicine. 2009. "Deafness in Disguise: Concealed Hearing Devices of the 19th and 20th Centuries. Washington University School of Medicine. Last modified June 15. http://beckerexhibits.wustl.edu/did/index.htm.

Wright, Kieth C., and Judith F. Davie. 1991. *Serving the Disabled: A How-To-Do-It Manual for Librarians*. New York: Neal-Schuman.

Keeping Assistive Technology Up-to-Date

It is almost never sufficient to consider assistive technology as a one-time purchase. New product releases, modification to the library's computer systems, and clarified or changing patron needs can all trigger reconsideration of the accommodations you provide.

Your library may already be doing some type of evaluation, for the library as a whole or for specific projects, and for a variety of reasons: justifying spending that has already occurred, making a case for new funding, identifying priorities, and so on. Probably staff members are already tracking technology requests from the public and evaluating new product releases for potential purchase. This chapter looks at ways to include assistive technology in these processes to ensure that your services continue to be relevant and useful for your patrons and defensible to other stakeholders.

Part of updating also involves being aware of trends both in general technology use and in assistive technology provision. The chapter ends with a look into the future and its potential impacts on your services to users with disabilities.

Why Upgrade?

There are two main types of reasons to consider upgrading your assistive technology:

- *Voluntary.* Voluntary upgrades are usually service-driven. They are responsive to patterns of need that have been identified during an evaluation or to user requests. However, they may also be due to new products or product versions that could be beneficial to your users.

- *Involuntary.* This can occur when the rest of the library's technology is upgraded or otherwise modified. Because your assistive technology may not work in this new situation, it will be necessary to consider the need for upgrades so that your services can continue with minimal interruption.

Each of these is discussed in more detail in the following sections.

Voluntary Upgrades

Evaluation, user demand, and release of new or upgraded products can all trigger a voluntary upgrade to your assistive computer technology services:

- *Evaluation.* In Chapter 1, we defined measurable objectives. Here, you will be gathering quantifiable information to support them. For example, if one of your goals is the outcome "65 percent of target patrons can now access e-mail," the evaluation process will let you determine whether this goal was met. Once this information is collected and analyzed, you may see specific actions to address, whether right away or in the next planning phase. We will look at considerations relevant to evaluating your assistive technology services.

- *User demand.* Users may take an active role in requesting accommodations other than those you currently offer. We will look at a strategy for evaluating user demand and responding appropriately.

- *New or upgraded products.* Like other for-profit manufacturers, assistive technology developers are likely to release periodic upgrades to their existing products as well as entirely new products. This will primarily apply to software, although consideration of hardware may be appropriate as well. The process for evaluating these can be similar to that used to review user requests.

Evaluation

The evaluation process should collect two types of quantifiable evidence: objective, or hard data about assistive technology use, and subjective, primarily feedback from end users. Your process of collecting and analyzing this evidence should be focused on appraising how well your goals were met and looking for evidence of what your next goals should be. However, it should also leave room for recording unexpected results, both positive and negative.

Objective Evidence

Donald A. Barclay, in his book *Managing Public-Access Computers*, talks about three ways of quantifying workstation usage: sign in/out systems, observation, and tracking software (Barclay, 2000). With assistive technology, there may be two other sources of evaluation information: patron registration and checkouts of assistive hardware.

- *Sign in/out systems.* If use of specific computers is restricted to individuals with disabilities who have registered with the library, reviewing information from manual or electronic sign in/out systems will provide input on how often these computers are used and the days and times they are used most often. The person doing the evaluation should receive information only about *when* the computers were used, not by whom.

Naturally, you will also want to make sure that people with disabilities are included in any general surveys of library users. Share information about accessibility with the people doing the survey, including both format options and accommodations such as use of a limited number of questions phrased in simple, straightforward language. The public at large is likely to benefit from the latter as well.

- *Observation.* This should be relatively unobtrusive. Library staff members can walk by the assistive technology workstations at an appointed time, note what accommodations (if any) are being used, go back to their desk, and record their notes. A sample sheet to record observations of assistive technology use appears below. Note that it uses pictures of hardware; you could also use typical screens from magnification options or a screen shot of a product's interface. This eliminates the need for observers to memorize product names.

    Observation will be mostly useful for hardware and third-party assistive technologies. It will not provide information on use of most accessibility system settings, such as StickyKeys; you may need to get information about these as part of the subjective evidence collection.

    Observation can occur on an ongoing basis, or during a specific time period—one week per month, two weeks twice a year, and so forth (Rhea Joyce Rubin, personal communication, September 2010). Observers should receive brief training on recognizing the specific software being evaluated. To get a comprehensive picture, make sure that the observations take place at different times each day during the observation period.

Sample Sheet for Recording Observations on Assistive Technology Use

Observation of Assistive Technology Computer Use

Date:	Time:
Computer #:	Observer:

Was the computer being used? _____ Yes _____ No

Was the patron wearing headphones? _____ Yes _____ No

Was the patron using a scanner? _____ Yes _____ No

Was the patron using any of the hardware pictured below? Check the blanks next to as many devices as relevant:

Was the text on the screen magnified? _____ Yes _____ No

Check the blank next to the description of the view that *most closely* resembles what you saw:

_____ Everything magnified   _____ Some things magnified

_____ Only document text magnified   _____ None of these

Did you see any of the icons shown below on the screen? _____ Yes _____ No

Thanks for your help!

- *Tracking software*, which records user activity in real time, might seem to be the easiest evaluation strategy. In reality, it has numerous complications that will make its use unlikely. Two of these are outlined by Donald A. Barclay (e-mail communication, July 26, 2010):

  1. Tracking software certainly does raise privacy issues. . . . The current thinking is that to track users at the clickstream level, you need to get them to agree to it up front. Without obtaining user consent, typically via an "I agree" pop up, tracking enters the realm of spying. . . . [I]n general the privacy concerns seem to have thrown a wet blanket on the use of tracking technology, at least for libraries.

  2. When you look at the marketing materials put out by companies that make tracking software (and flat-out spyware), their customer base appears to be 100% commercial—Web retailers, marketers, etc. Privacy concerns aside, the cost of tracking software may put it out of reach of most libraries.

- *Patron registration*. If your library policy asks patrons with disabilities to complete a registration form before they can use assistive computer technology, at a minimum you should be able to determine the total number of registrations. You may also be able to glean other information from these forms—for example, demographics for various types of disabilities, which may provide insight into the technology likely to be used most often. In any case, protection of user privacy should be paramount.

- *Checkouts*. Checkout information about specialized keyboards and mice can easily be incorporated into your evaluation. Checkout of more mainstream peripherals, such as headsets or scanners, can be trickier, because people may use these with software other than assistive technology. For these peripherals, you could designate specific units that are used only with the assistive technology machines or include their use as part of the observation process. To protect privacy, make sure that any identifying information, such as name or drivers' license/state ID number, is not recorded on the checkout sheet or is blacked out before being given to the person doing the evaluation.

Subjective Evidence

Your evaluation process will also benefit from having quantifiable subjective feedback from users. This can be accomplished via the same strategies you used when planning—surveys, interviews, focus groups, and so forth—although you will want a wider sample than just the people who were involved in the planning. If you register users with disabilities and/or collect contact information for attendees at assistive technology–related events and have gotten format preferences for feedback collection (see pp. 5–8), you already have an identifiable group of people to involve in this process. Otherwise, you could use methods of feedback solicitation that have proven useful with a general audience or other target groups. You could also involve your community partners,

Pop-ups can cause barriers for assistive technology users, because these may appear before their technology has started, may not be readable by this technology, or may start reading information for which the user does not have a context.

focus group members, and identified community leaders in recruiting participants. Consider providing an incentive for participation, for example, a small giveaway or entry into a raffle for a larger prize. Be sure to provide clear information about why you are asking for feedback, such as, "We are collecting information to help determine our assistive technology funding priorities for next year."

Start the feedback process by asking people what technologies they have been using. It may be more effective to ask about the purpose of the equipment used (magnification, "blind access," etc.) than to list exact products. As with the observation tool, it may be useful to include pictures of the hardware or a sample screen shot of the software. Leave open possibilities for scenarios such as patrons with disabilities being attracted to the library computer lab by the presence of assistive technologies but discovering that they did not need these technologies to successfully use a computer.

Your next step is to ask about patrons' perceived results from using assistive computer technology. The Sample Computer Use Survey (p. 106) is designed to collect information relevant to the goals you're measuring. You might also want to ask more general questions about topics such as opinions on the technology or how easy it is for them to get computer time. Consider changing the tone of the survey depending on your audience; for example, the sample survey assumes a group of patrons with disabilities who are mostly computer neophytes, but you may know that most of the target audience members in your library are experienced computer users who simply need accommodations to use the library's computing services. If you have added materials or done programming related to assistive technology, you may want to add questions to your survey that measure the effectiveness of these services as well.

You may also want to gather information from internal stakeholders, particularly front-line staff and members of the IT department. Because these stakeholders will be wary of sharing information that they feel may compromise their jobs, this process should use collection strategies that maximize anonymity, such as online surveys. Ask them about both their own experiences (e.g., do front-line staff members feel that trainings adequately prepared them to provide services to people with disabilities? Do IT staff members find that setting up assistive technology requires an inordinate amount of time or less time than expected?) and about any observations they had related to end users' experiences.

Presenting Results

> If assessment is intended to produce information for political decision-making, the library has to determine who its political audiences are and what they most want to know. What the audiences want to know may well be different from what the library thinks they need to know. (Childers and Van House, 1993: 54)

As you assemble your results, think about their impact. At a minimum, this will involve identifying your audiences (the individuals or groups who want or need to know the results of your evaluation), what each

> Make sure that you're using the same accessibility considerations for collecting information that you used in the planning step (see Chapter 1, pp. 5–8).

Sample Computer Use Survey

Date:

Do you use specialized equipment at the library to help you use the computer?

☐ Yes   ☐ No

If "yes," please provide the name or a description of the equipment (e.g., "magnification" or "big keyboard"):

Before using the library computers, did you feel you could use a computer?

☐ Yes   ☐ No

Comments:

Do you feel confident now about your ability to use computers in the library?

☐ Yes   ☐ No

Comments:

Do you feel confident now about your ability to use computers in other locations?

☐ Yes   ☐ No

Comments:

Which of the following are you able to do now that you couldn't do before using the library's computers? Please check all that apply:

☐ Access e-mail   ☐ Look up information   ☐ Other:

☐ Write letters, school papers, etc.   ☐ Access the online library catalog

Comments:

Do you feel you have more social connections as a result of using the library's computers?

☐ Yes   ☐ No

Comments:

As a result of using the library's computers, were you able to do any of the following? (Check all that apply.)

☐ Apply for a job   ☐ Apply for government benefits   ☐ Other:

☐ Go back to school   ☐ Carry out personal tasks like paying bills

Comments:

Is there anything else you'd like us to know?

Thanks for your time!

EVALUATION IN ACTION

Calgary Public Library

You may wish to evaluate and modify your other services to individuals with disabilities as well. In 2000, Rosemary Griebel from the Calgary (AB, Canada) Public Library published an article in the *PNLA Quarterly* about services libraries across Canada were providing to print-disabled individuals in collaboration with the Canadian National Institute for the Blind (CNIB); the issue is available at http://www.pnla.org/quarterly/Fall2000/Final%20Fall%202000%20PNLA.pdf.

In response to my inquiry about how these services have changed in the past ten years, Heather Robertson, the manager of Diversity Services for the Calgary Public Library, provided the following update:

CNIB VISUNET Canada Partners Program

Much about CPL's relationship with the CNIB Library and participation in the VISUNET: Canada Partners program remains the same:

- Provides seamless service—customers who are blind or visually impaired, as well as the larger audience of people with print disabilities, can visit their local library and access the VISUNET: Canada resources as well as other sources of alternate formats (both available in-house and as part of our provincial-wide consortium Alberta Library (TAL).
- CPL customers who have a print disability have access to the VISUCAT online catalogue, VISUNEWS, and VISUTEXT services provided by the VISUNET: Canada Partners program.
- VISUNET: Canada Partners program provides CPL with a small traveling collection of talking books for distribution to customers at the local level. This collection is refreshed every 4 months.

There have also been a few changes:

- March 2007—CNIB ceased production of the Talking Book cassette format in favour of a new, higher quality, audio format—DAISY. CNIB no longer carries the TKBK cassette format and is rapidly working to build up their DAISY collection.
- 2009—CNIB Library launched a funding campaign with provincial and federal governments, requesting funding support for the continuation of the VISUNET: Canada Partners program. CNIB is funded largely by charitable donations and in recent years the increasing number of clients and libraries accessing CNIB services has created funding challenges that needed to be addressed. Alberta was the first province to join the VISUNET: Canada Partners program and, in fact, was the province that had a hand in developing the program initially, and therefore provided the funding support requested.
- March 2010—Because of continued funding challenges, CNIB cancelled the Public Library sales program that enabled local libraries to purchase permanent collections of TKBK formats for local library distribution. This had an impact on the breadth and depth of alternate formats available to customers with print disabilities within their local library locations. Customers still have access to VISUNET resources, but resources are available only on request.

Changes in the delivery of Special Services at CPL:

- Implementation of the ALEX (Adaptive Technology Workstation) in 2002. This station is composed of a number of adaptive hardware and software components to enable a customer of any age or ability to access the Internet and online productivity tools. CPL also provides a number of other assistive technology tools including Assistive Listening devices, Reading machine, CCTV, magnifying glasses, etc.
- Provision of materials in alternate formats including:
  - Large Print collection
  - Audiobooks available in Booktape (no longer available as of 2010), BookCD, and MP3 formats. Materials are both abridged and unabridged and purchased directly through publishing companies as titles are available. A collection of unabridged audiobooks in MP3 format are set aside for customers with print disabilities to complement the DAISY collection purchased or loaned through the VISUNET: Canada Partners program.
  - Downloadable e-book and audiobook formats
  - Descriptive video collection

(Continued)

○ In order for customers to benefit from the full navigational features of the DAISY format, they must play the material on a VICTOR player. Therefore, CPL provides a small collection of VICTOR players that customers can loan to try out the DAISY format. Library staff will also refer customers to the CNIB or companies like HumanWare to purchase their own players.

CPL also continues to offer programs in support of people with health or mobility concerns including:

- Homebound Readers Program—library volunteers bring library resources directly to customers who are unable to visit the library themselves due to health or mobility concerns.
- Libraries in Residence—library staff select and deliver "mini libraries" to continuing care centers and seniors' residences. Volunteers host the in-residence libraries or provide "room-service" via book trolleys.
- In-Home Computer Help—volunteers will visit customers in their home to provide one-on-one coaching sessions that help people become comfortable using the Internet, e-mail, and software applications.

Challenges to service?

- Increasing amount of material being made in downloadable, electronic format only. This provides implications for customers who may not have access to a computer or who may have difficulty in using computer technology. This also reduces the amount of physical formats that public libraries can make available for loan by customers.

(*Source*: Heather Robertson, e-mail communication, September 8, 2010.)

audience needs to know, what they will likely do with the information, and how the information should be delivered (Rubin, 2006).

A primary audience will likely be some type of current or potential funding resource, whether the Friends of the Library or other source that provided specific monies for assistive technology implementation or the library's overall budget managers. They will want proof that the money allocated to assistive technology was well spent; you will want to be able to use that proof when asking for additional funds.

Consider internal stakeholders as well. Library administration and board members will be interested in proof that time and effort was well spent to address the needs of an underserved population. Another important audience may be your IT staff, who will benefit from assurance that the work they have done to implement assistive technology has paid off. Their primary interest may be in statistics, although anecdotal information may be useful to them as well.

External stakeholders will include anyone potentially affected by or interested in your services. An obvious audience includes patrons, your funders, your collaborators, and other community groups. Other audience members may range from members of your local government's Commission on Disabilities to libraries that are interested in your experiences as a model for implementation.

Sooner or later, you may also need to structure your results to see if they can make an argument for or against specific actions. For example, if library management decides that four hours per week need to be cut from your schedule of open hours, they may be looking for input on the best time slot to do this. If your results show that Monday afternoons and Friday mornings show a significant spike in assistive technology usage, that could be an effective argument for not cutting hours during those times.

If you need to provide a report, it will likely present information in two ways: as statistics (aggregated information) and as anecdotes (information volunteered by individuals in response to open-ended questions). Each will have its role in presenting clear, accurate evidence about the effectiveness of your services.

Ideally, your information collection process will have made report writing fairly easy. A sample template for organizing quantifiable data (including any quantifiable results that can be drawn from user feedback, e.g., number of patrons who say they use a specific program) appears below. You will want to append separate pages that have the results of users' narrative responses.

If you are just evaluating your assistive technology services, or your overall services to people with disabilities, it's likely that you can find existing assessment templates that are worded broadly enough to be useful in generating your final report. If you are not already involved in your library's overall evaluation processes, find someone who is and ask him or her for copies of templates that have been effective or reports that were well received.

If, instead, your assistive technology evaluation is part of the library's assessment of its entire functionality, you may need to add assistive technology-related categories to the overall template being used. Think about whether these categories would be more effective listed under evaluation of technology services or services to target populations. Word them in accordance with the goals that you set during planning, for example, "Increased library attendance by people with disabilities" or "Enhanced development of computer use skills."

> Be careful how you use anecdotes. Do they help portray real progress in achieving goals, or do they just tell a "heartwarming" story?

Sample Sheet for Summarizing Evaluation Information

Date:	Evaluator:
Evaluation Start Date:	Evaluation End Date:

Aggregated Results

From registration records:
    Number of patrons with disabilities registered to use assistive computer tech =
    Number registered during prior evaluation period =
    Percentage change =

From sign-in records:
    Number of times patrons signed in to use adapted computers =

From observation and/or tracking software:
    Number of times patrons used Software A =
    Number of times patrons used Software B =
    Number of times patrons used Software C =
    Number of times patrons used Software D =

(Continued)

Sample Sheet for Summarizing Evaluation Information *(Continued)*

Aggregated Results *(Continued)*

From observation and/or tracking software:

  Number of times patrons used Software A =
  Number of times patrons used Software B =
  Number of times patrons used Software C =
  Number of times patrons used Software D =

From checkout records:

  Number of times patrons used Hardware A =
  Number of times patrons used Hardware B =
  Number of times patrons used Hardware C =

From user feedback:

  Number of patrons who use assistive tech =
  Number of patrons who say they use Software A =
  Number of patrons who say they use Software B =
  Number of patrons who say they use Software C =
  Number of patrons who say they use Software D =
  Number of patrons who say they use Hardware A =
  Number of patrons who say they use Hardware B =
  Number of patrons who say they use Hardware C =

Outcome Information

  Number of patrons who felt confident using computers before using the library =
  Number of patrons who felt confident using computers after using the library, but not before =
  Number of patrons who still don't feel confident using computers =
  Number of patrons who can now access e-mail =
  Number of patrons who can now use the computers for writing =
  Number of patrons who can now look up information =
  Number of patrons who can now access the online catalog =

  Other tasks listed by patrons and numbers who can now do them:

  Number of patrons who reported having more social connections as a result of using computers =
  Number of patrons who did not report having more social connections =

  Number of patrons who applied for a job =
  Number of patrons who went back to school =
  Number of patrons who applied for gov't benefits =
  Number of patrons who carried out personal tasks =

  Other accomplishments listed by patrons and numbers who achieved them:

Keeping Assistive Technology Up-to-Date

Acting On Results

Think of the completion of the report as the beginning of the next round of planning. The advantage of this round is that you'll have a wide variety of specific information to draw on. Have community needs seemed to change? Are there products whose popularity suggests the need for additional copies? Have one or more of your goals not been met or become obsolete? Are there unexpected results, and what responses do they seem to require?

Some results may require immediate action, such as complaints about an inaccessible pathway between the accessible computer workstations and the bathroom. Others will present a clear priority for the next round of planning or funding or show the effectiveness of your existing program. The Priority Worksheet discussed later in the "User Demand" section may be helpful for reviewing equipment requests that come out of the evaluation process.

However, you are also likely to have results for which creative responses may be needed. For example, your evaluation may show that large LCD monitors are used by 85 percent of your patrons with disabilities, and they would like them to be available on every accessible computer, but you're unlikely to fit this into your budget for some time. The situation can be described to one or more appropriate stakeholders—your focus group members, your IT department, your community partners, the vendors you've worked with, and so on—for discussion and brainstorming of solutions. You might find that a community partner is willing to add a large print monitor to one of their public access computers or a that a focus group member knows someone looking to recycle a 20" monitor in good condition.

User Demand

Think of demand as ongoing user self-evaluation: patrons with disabilities have learned that you're implementing some type of assistive technology program, and they want to make sure your services meet their particular needs and goals. This should be encouraged because it's an easy way to get information that can predict, supplement, or become part of the results of your evaluation.

Find out all the ways that your library receives and records unsolicited user input: suggestion boxes, tracking of phone calls and e-mails, and so on. Post information about all of these options prominently on your website, and distribute this information when you register people as assistive technology users, when you provide programs, and so on.

Make sure that all staff members know that any comments related to assistive technology should go to the staff member responsible for its implementation. These comments should then be reviewed, ideally by at least two staff members, to discuss implications. Then, they should be sorted into requests that require a quick response, such as a complaint about a broken computer, and those that will need to be evaluated to demonstrate a pattern, such as requests for specific hardware or software.

Periodically aggregate technology requests. Then, for each requested technology, assess them using a tool such as the Priority Worksheet on page 113. This worksheet helps you assign a score to each of four considerations:

- *Demand.* This simply measures the number of requests for a given technology. The numbers on the sample worksheet can be adjusted based on your demographics.

- *Impact.* How likely is this technology to be relevant to users who haven't requested it? Review Chapter 2 and determine whether the technology is relevant only to a narrow group of users or if it can be used to meet a wide variety of needs. The larger the potential user base, the higher the score. If appropriate, also consider whether the technology works with only one or two of the mainstream applications you offer or with most or all of these applications. The numbers on the sample worksheet can be adjusted if necessary or changed to a word-based scale (e.g., "No other users, Many other users").

- *Cost.* This measures the upfront cost of the technology. The less expensive the technology, the higher the score it receives. These numbers can be adjusted based on your budget.

- *Maintenance.* This measures the hidden costs of the technology for both the library and the end users—complexity of installation, learning curve, amount of time necessary for users to set up their configuration preferences before each computer session, compatibility issues with existing technology, and so on. Reviewing Chapter 2 and deciding which category this technology belongs to may help with the maintenance evaluation. You will probably also need to do additional research and talk to IT staff before assigning this score. Again, lower maintenance costs should result in higher scores.

Decide ahead of time what the scores will mean. For example, a score of 15 or higher may mean the technology is an automatic priority for the next round of funding, while a score of 10–14 means that it receives a lower priority but is still worth working into the budget if possible. For a technology that receives scores lower than 10, think about whether you want to score it on a cumulative average based on multiple evaluation periods or whether each technology is scored on only the current round of input.

For example: you notice that during a four-month period, nine users have asked for "Wally's Wonder Widget," a software program that magnifies individual cells in Excel spreadsheets. The software could be scored as follows:

- Assign 3 Demand points for the number of requests. You might or might not decide to add additional points representing requests for the program that you received in the past.

- Magnification can be of use to a large number of individuals. However, you already know from other surveys, which included

Priority Worksheet for Considering Purchase of New Assistive Technology

Date: /   /

Name of Technology:
Ordering Information:

Demand (number of users who requested the technology):

☐ 1	☐ 2–4	☐ 5–10	☐ 11–14	☐ 15 or more
Score: 1	Score: 2	Score: 3	Score: 4	Score: 5

Comments:

Impact (number of additional users likely to benefit from the technology):

☐ 0	☐ 1–4	☐ 5–10	☐ 11–14	☐ 15 or more
Score: 1	Score: 2	Score: 3	Score: 4	Score: 5

Comments:

Cost (upfront cost):

☐ $150/more	☐ $100–$149	☐ $50–$99	☐ $1–$49	☐ Free
Score: 1	Score: 2	Score: 3	Score: 4	Score: 5

Comments:

Maintenance (hidden costs):

☐ Very high	☐ High	☐ Average	☐ Low	☐ Very low
Score: 1	Score: 2	Score: 3	Score: 4	Score: 5

Comments:

Total score:

people with disabilities, that only about 10 percent of the library's patrons use Excel. You decide to score the Impact as 3.

- The program costs $129, so it receives a Cost score of 2.
- You find out that the program is easy to activate from the Excel menu bar. IT reports that this shouldn't interfere with security software or cause other problems. You assign a Maintenance score of 4.

The total score for Wally's Wonder Widget is therefore 12, meaning that it's not a top priority but is still worth including in funding considerations.

Ideally, your library already has mechanisms for letting users know about responses to their requests. Take advantage of this so that patrons with disabilities know that even if you decide not to purchase the item they requested, it at least received fair consideration.

New Products and New Releases

Assistive technology programs are like any other software when it comes to new products or product upgrades: sometimes there are enhanced capabilities, and sometimes more problems are caused than solved. Use of a tool such as the Priority Worksheet can be used to make decisions about whether or not to acquire these programs.

As previously noted, most vendors offer free demos of their products, usually via download from their website. It should be easy in most cases to get a demo and show it to IT staff to help assess its hidden costs. Then use the Priority Worksheet to assign Cost and Maintenance scores. For products that receive promising scores in these areas, invite a vendor or user to provide a demonstration to your patrons, and collect feedback on whether they feel the product is worth acquiring. Use this to determine Demand and Impact scores.

Another way to help decide whether to upgrade a product would be to add a "Value of Upgrade" item to the Priority Worksheet. This item could run from "Very low value" (score: 1) to "Very high value" (score: 5). Value could be calculated on a variety of factors, including:

- addition of *useful* features (mere addition of features should not be the sole criteria);
- number of bug fixes (usually listed in a "Read Me" or "What's New" document, on the manufacturers website or as part of the program's documentation);
- an easier to use interface; and
- added or enhanced compatibility with mainstream programs the library provides to the public, for example, support for a new version of a browser.

The maximum score for a product would then become 25; you might decide that, say, 18 would be the cutoff score for purchasing an upgrade.

Assistive technology hardware is less likely to have significant upgrades to specific models. There may, however, be new models worth considering; for example, an adjustable keyboard that has proven popular may also become available as a smaller sized unit or with additional adjustment options. You can use the Priority Worksheet to evaluate these as you would for software.

Involuntary Upgrades

Software

In the early days of personal computing, there could be gaps of several months or even years between the release of a new operating system and the corresponding release of compatible assistive technology. This was

> Major changes to the interface that don't seem to improve the functionality or the ease of use should, in most cases, cause you to score the upgrade's value lower rather than higher. Having to learn a new interface without receiving significant benefits can be extremely frustrating to users.

particularly true in the latter half of the 1980s, as Microsoft moved from the text-based DOS operating systems to the more graphic Windows interface. Fortunately, this is now far less true; if compatible versions of assistive software aren't available the same day as the operating system is released, they're usually not far behind.

If your library is upgrading to a new operating system, it's possible there may not be a compatibility issue with your existing software. Assistive software developers are generally reliable about posting compatibility information to their website before or shortly after a new operating system is released. Keep track of this information and call the vendor if you have any questions. Also keep your IT contacts in the loop so that they will know they should reinstall the programs they already have.

It's also possible that there may be a patch available that can be added to your existing software to achieve compatibility. These are usually free and downloadable from the developer's website. Gather as much information as you can about this patch—URL and system requirements, at a minimum—and work with your IT contacts to get it downloaded and installed.

In the worst case, you may need to purchase a new version of the product in question when it becomes available. If your evaluation results showed dissatisfaction with the product, this may be a good excuse to consider buying a competing product instead.

If you're relying on built-in system features to meet some or all of your assistive technology needs, be aware that when these change from system to system, it's not always for the better. An example of this situation is the declining usefulness of the Display settings in Windows (see pp. 20–21). You may need to consider buying a third-party product to restore at least some of the capabilities that your patrons have become accustomed to using.

> Some assistive technology software may have a limit on the number of times it can be installed. If you've already reached this limit, you may not be able to reinstall it on new or upgraded computers. A call to the manufacturer explaining the situation will usually result in their issuing a new installation code or other means of ensuring that you can activate the software on your new systems.

Hardware

Your existing assistive hardware may not work with your new computers for the reasons noted in Chapter 4: incompatible drivers or connectors. Check with the manufacturers for their advice, and consider replacing your old equipment with competing products if necessary and available. At a minimum, keep in touch with vendors to let them know you represent part of the demand for updated compatibility and that you would like to be notified whenever an upgrade becomes available.

The Future

Technology trends change much faster than people do. New devices will not immediately gain acceptance and superannuate your existing computer lab. However, libraries are already starting to purchase computer alternatives such as e-readers and tablets, and many users will bring in their own equipment. Ideally, your assistive technology services can automatically become one of the ongoing considerations in the evolution of your library's overall technology program.

Video game machines are also becoming available in some libraries. Fortunately, in many cases innovations in gaming have dovetailed well with increased out-of-the-box accessibility. The Kinect, the first gaming system that doesn't require use of a controller, has tremendous potential for many types of users. For example, at least one four-year-old with autism found it entirely intuitive to use (Yan, 2010), and researchers at New York University are working to create software that allows the Kinect to be used as an input device for a man with minimal movement and very low vision (Newman, Kazansky, and Jennings, 2011).

The Near Future: Personal Technology

Libraries are moving from providing only desktop computers to installing wireless services that let people access the Internet using a wide variety of devices. In some instances, this will be ideal for accommodation—people with disabilities probably already have any devices they own configured to their preferences, and mainstream devices such as the iPad increasingly have assistive technology options either built in or available as downloadable applications ("apps"). However, there are at least three issues to consider before deciding to reduce or eliminate your existing assistive computer technology services:

- *Compatibility.* People are likely to bring a wide range of technologies to your library. Some of these may work fine with your WiFi or other connection setup, others may have periodic problems, and still others may not work at all. As a backup, you will need to ensure an alternative method for people to connect to the Internet. This will likely be via either your existing computer lab or portable devices acquired and provided by the library.

- *Alternatives.* Many people won't have personal devices or will choose not to bring them to the library for reasons including weight, fear of technology being damaged or stolen, and so on. Others may have strong preferences for using technologies that are already familiar to them, including assistive technologies, and may resist using any new products.

- *Broader purposes.* The evaluation of your assistive technology program, or another library evaluation, may show that your patrons see the computer lab as having functions other than simply providing access to a computer. For example, as Brian Hawkins and Diane Oblinger (2007: 11) wrote about academic computer labs, "Public clusters provide more than just access to the technology. These are 'social places' where students can collaborate and share expertise, both technical and disciplinary. Labs may even be used off-hours for entertainment (e.g., LAN parties or gaming tournaments)." Whatever the nature of these functions, they will need to remain accessible to people with disabilities, with assistive technology assuming its proper role.

As services are modified, remember that there will still need to be at least one staff member who is versed in the accessibility implications of newly acquired technologies. Plan job assignments and trainings accordingly.

Down the Road: The Global Public Inclusive Infrastructure

Imagine being a person with a disability who's able to go into any library or other public computing facility, enter a code into any Internet-connected device, and instantly have your preferred assistive technology come up with your settings activated. You're complacent about this, because the same capability is also available from devices such as the kiosks you use when shopping and your newly purchased smartphone.

Unlikely? Not according to Jim Fruchterman and Gregg Vanderheiden, who are working to build a Global Public Inclusive Infrastructure (GPII). The advent of "cloud computing," where resources are stored on the Internet rather than on individual machines, makes this technically feasible; any device connected to the Internet will have the potential to take advantage of this service. Anyone will be able to use the basic GPII services for free, while those willing and able to pay could have access to more advanced options that have, say, better quality voices or advanced features. More details about this initiative are available at http://raising thefloor.net/ and http://gpii.org/.

Gregg Vanderheiden (personal communication, September 25, 2010, and March 23, 2011) believes libraries "will be key" in both the testing and provision of GPII services and "will also benefit materially from the GPII." The project envisions a world where the following will be possible for all users with disabilities, including an elder named Ernesto:

> When someone goes into any [library] for the first time the staff can take them over to any available computer and activate the personalization wizard on the web. The staff can then walk away and this friendly, and actually fun, program goes through and talks (using speech, captions, and sign language) and shows the person different access features and technologies and finds out what works best for them. When that's done, it automatically stores what the person needs somewhere where they can use it anywhere, any time. Now when that person sits down to any computer, at any of the libraries, the computers automatically and instantly change into the form that they need. Ernesto doesn't understand how—it is all like magic. But now he can go to the library just like his friends that don't need special adaptations. And they all just sit down at any computer and he can use it just like they can. (Global Public Inclusive Infrastructure, 2010)

Summary and Conclusion

Congratulations! In this chapter, you reviewed the work you've done to make your library computers accessible to people with disabilities and gotten a perspective on how to keep this important service going well into the future. Your evaluation will likely show that your services to people with disabilities have become important enough to be considered as an ongoing part of the library's overall planning, budgeting, and functionality.

However, assistive technology provision is unlikely to thrive on an ongoing basis if only one person is championing it. That person may leave, have his or her job duties reassigned, or change his or her involvement for another reason. At a minimum, make sure that there is clearly organized information that can be passed on to the next person responsible for the technology. Keep copies of the worksheets that you've used from this book to provide guidance on why particular products were and weren't selected and what products should be considered first in upcoming budgets. Also include contact information for focus group members, point people at your community partner organizations, funding resources, and vendors with whom there has been a successful relationship.

Quality assistive technology provision should meet the same hallmarks as any other library function. A majority of patrons should have their needs met, staff should feel comfortable that they are sufficiently well-informed to provide high levels of service, and funding should be directed where it can be shown to do the most good. Part of ensuring this is to circulate information among library professionals about what has and hasn't worked in specific settings. If you would like to share stories of your experience, e-mail me at jane@janevincent.com and I will add them to this book's blog at http://www.janevincent.com/iceact.

▶ **Companion Blog**

For resource updates, visit this book's companion blog at http://www.janevincent.com/iceact.

References

Barclay, Donald A. 2000. *Managing Public-Access Computers.* New York: Neal Schuman.

Childers, Thomas A., and Nancy A. Van House. 1993. *What's Good? Describing Your Public Library's Effectiveness.* Chicago: American Library Association.

Global Public Inclusive Infrastructure (GPII). 2010. "Today and Tomorrow." GPII. http://npii.org/todayandtomorrow.

Hawkins, Brian L., and Diane G. Oblinger. 2007. "The Myth about the Need for Public Computer Labs." *EDUCAUSE Review* 42, no. 7, September/October: 10–11.

Newman, Erica, Rebecca Kazansky, and William Jennings. 2011. "Sign Wave." Tisch ITP (New York University). http://itp.nyu.edu/shows/spring2011/2011/05/01/sign-wave/.

Rubin, Rhea Joyce. 2006. *Demonstrating Results: Using Outcome Measurement in Your Library.* Chicago: American Library Association.

Yan, John. 2010. "I Think Kinect Is OK, but It's the Best $150 I Spent on a Console." *Gaming Nexus* (blog), November 9. http://www.gamingnexus.com/FullNews/I-think-Kinect-is-OK2c-but-its-the-best-24150-I-spent-on-a-console/Item20369.aspx.

Assistive Technology Manufacturers, Vendors, and Websites

Appendix

Notes:

- This list is neither exhaustive nor intended to provide endorsements. It simply lists manufacturers and vendors that are well established and that have products relevant to the categories discussed in Chapter 2. As with any other type of sales, specific products may be discontinued, and companies may merge or go out of business. For the most up-to-date information, and for products not covered by the companies in this list, you should check Abledata (http://www.able data.com/) and the other resources listed in Chapter 3 (pp. 51–52).

- Assistive technology manufacturers primarily develop and sell their own products; vendors primarily sell products from multiple manufacturers. However, there are some vendors who develop a few of their own products and some manufacturers who also sell products from other sources.

Manufacturers of Assistive Technology

AD-AS (adjustable tables)
2720 West Idaho Street
Boise, ID 83702
800-957-2720
http://www.ad-as.com/

Ai Squared (magnification software)
P.O. Box 669
Manchester Center, VT 05255
800-859-0270
http://www.aisquared.com/

Dolphin Computer Access, Inc. (screen reader, magnification)
231 Clarksville Road, Suite 3
Princeton Junction, NJ 08550
866-797-5921
http://www.yourdolphin.com/?lang2=en&loc=US

Don Johnston, Inc. (software for comprehension barriers)
26799 West Commerce Drive
Volo, IL 60073
800-999-4660
http://www.donjohnston.com/

Freedom Scientific Blind/Low Vision Group (screen reader, magnification)
11800 31st Court North
St. Petersburg, FL 33716-1805
800-444-4443
http://www.freedomscientific.com/

Freedom Scientific Learning Systems Group (software for comprehension barriers)
11800 31st Court North
St. Petersburg, FL 33716-1805
800-444-4443
http://www.freedomscientific.com/LSG

Goldtouch (alternative keyboards)
1101 Arrow Point Drive, Bldg. 4, Suite 401
Cedar Park, TX 78613
877-235-5885
http://goldtouch.com/

GW Micro, Inc. (screen reader)
725 Airport North Office Park
Fort Wayne, IN 46825
260-489-3671
http://www.gwmicro.com/

Intellitools (alternative keyboard and software for comprehension barriers)
4185 Salazar Way
Frederick, CO 80504
800-547-6747
http://www.intellitools.com/

Kensington Computer Products Group (alternative mice)
333 Twin Dolphin Drive, Sixth Floor
Redwood Shores, CA 94065
650-572-2700
http://us.kensington.com/

Kinesis Corporation (alternative keyboards)
22121 17th Avenue SE, Suite 112
Bothell, WA 98021-7404
800-454-6374
http://www.kinesis.com/

Kurzweil Educational Systems (software for comprehension and monitor barriers)
A Cambium Learning Technologies Company
24 Prime Parkway, Suite 303

Natick, MA 01760
800-547-6747
http://www.kurzweiledu.com/

Madentec Ltd. (keyboard/mouse alternatives)
4664 99 Street
Edmonton, Alberta, Canada T6E 5H5
780-450-8926
http://www.madentec.com/

Nuance Communications, Inc. (voice recognition)
1 Wayside Road
Burlington, MA 01803
800-654-1187
http://www.nuance.com/

RJ Cooper & Assoc. (keyboard/mouse alternatives)
27601 Forbes Road, Suite 39
Laguna Niguel, CA 92677
800-752-6673
http://www.rjcooper.com/

TextHelp Systems, Inc. (software for comprehension barriers)
100 Unicorn Park Drive
Woburn, MA 01801
888-248-0652
http://www.texthelp.com/

Vendors

A.T. Kratter & Company, Inc.
12062 Valley View Street, Suite 109
Garden Grove, CA 92845-1739
714-799-3000
http://www.atkratter.com/

Access Ingenuity, Inc.
3635 Montgomery Drive
Santa Rosa, CA 95405
877-579-4380
http://www.accessingenuity.com/

Adaptive Solutions, Inc.
1301 Azalea Road, Suite 101
P.O. Box 191087
Mobile, AL 36619-1087
800-299-3045
http://www.talksight.com/

EnableMart
5353 South 960 East, Suite 200
Salt Lake City, UT 84117

888-640-1999
http://www.enablemart.com/

Infogrip, Inc.
1794 E. Main Street
Ventura, CA 93001
800-397-0921
http://www.infogrip.com/

Integration Technologies, Inc., Accessibility Solutions Group
2745 Hartland Road, 2nd Floor
Falls Church, VA 22043
703-698-8282
http://www.itgonline.com/accessibility-solutions.html

NanoPac, Inc.
4823 South Sheridan Road, Suite 302
Tulsa, OK 74145-5717
800-580-6086
http://www.nanopac.com/

Sterling Adaptives
7665 Redwood Blvd., Suite 100
Novato, CA 94945
415-878-2922
http://www.sterlingadaptives.com/

Websites Listing Accessibility Apps for iOS and Android Hardware

Apps4Android
http://apps4android.org/press-releases/apps4android_apps.htm
> This website tracks a variety of accessibility apps for the Android platform.

AT Mac
http://atmac.org/
> This exceptional website tracks accessibility related to all Apple products, including apps for iOS products (iPhone, iPad, and iTouch).

Christopher Reeve Foundation
http://tinyurl.com/2wxocvp
> The Christopher Reeve Foundation website lists accessibility apps of specific interest to people with paralysis, covering both the iOS and Android platforms.

Eyes-Free
http://eyes-free.googlecode.com/svn/trunk/documentation/android_access/apps.html
> This website lists a variety of Android apps that are screen-reader friendly.

Glossary

Note: Terms in SMALL CAPITAL LETTERS are defined elsewhere in the glossary.

accessible: Used to describe a product or environment that can be used by a majority of individuals with and without disabilities. In some situations, accessibility can be introduced or improved through use of ASSISTIVE TECHNOLOGY.

alternative formats: Generally used to refer to materials provided in other than standard-sized print. LARGE PRINT, BRAILLE, audio files, and electronic files that can be read by SCREEN READERS and TEXT READERS can all be considered alternative formats.

American Sign Language (ASL): The primary nonverbal language used by Deaf Americans. ASL has a sophisticated vocabulary and syntax and also incorporates facial expressions and other physical movements. Throughout the United States, several regional dialects of ASL are used.

Americans with Disabilities Act (ADA): A 1990 law that protects the civil rights of people with disabilities, where "disability" is defined as "a physical or mental impairment that substantially limits one or more major life activities of such individual." This book addresses a larger population than the ADA; for example, color blindness is not covered by the ADA, although color-blind people may benefit from ASSISTIVE TECHNOLOGY use. Title II of the ADA addresses "state and municipal entities," and Title III focuses on "places of public accommodation;" both titles will be relevant to most public libraries.

app: Short for "application," app is currently used to refer to programs run on SMARTPHONES, TABLETS, and other mobile devices. Apps are often developed by individuals who are not affiliated with traditional software companies.

assistive technology: In the context of this book, any product that makes a standard computer usable to one or more people with disabilities. In other contexts, it may also refer to products that help with other functions, from inexpensive pocket magnifiers to high-tech communication devices.

Blio: An e-book format designed to echo the layout of traditional books, including pictures. A built-in Read Aloud function will read some books aloud without requiring other adaptations. As of March 2011, any Blio book should be readable by most screen readers.

braille: A tactile reading format used by a minority of blind individuals, usually those who have been blind since childhood. Some systems of braille provide shorthand (e.g., contracting the suffix "ing" into a single letter) or are used for specialized vocabularies, such as mathematics.

carpal tunnel syndrome: *See* REPETITIVE STRAIN INJURY.

cognitively disabled: Generally used to refer to people with significantly below-average intelligence as measured by standard tests, although they may have average or above-average capabilities in other areas. It may also apply to individuals who have lost cognitive function because of a stroke, brain injury, or other cause. Compare with LEARNING DISABLED.

color blindness: Inability to distinguish between specific colors, most commonly red and green. In extreme cases, people with color blindness cannot perceive color at all. Color blindness affects far more men than women.

cursor: *See* POINTER.

DAISY: An E-BOOK format designed for maximal accessibility that includes both audio and visual files. Readers can access these files in a variety of ways, for example, by simultaneously listening to and reading text.

Deaf: When capitalized, "Deaf" refers to people who consider themselves part of a distinct cultural group. When in lower case, "deaf" refers to the medical condition of being unable to hear.

disability: In the context of this book, "disability" refers to any physical or cognitive condition that may affect someone's ability to use a standard computer. This includes youths, elders, and people with beginning literacy skills, as well as people with cerebral palsy, low vision, or Down syndrome.

drivers: Drivers are small software programs that serve as an interface between the computer and devices that are plugged into it—such as keyboards, mice, and printers—allowing them to work together smoothly.

Dvorak: An alternative keyboard layout designed to increase typing efficiency.

e-book: A book in one of several electronic formats. These formats may incorporate accessible features (e.g., the capability of reading aloud), may work with assistive technologies, or may be inaccessible.

e-reader: A device primarily used for reading E-BOOKS. As of this writing, the Amazon Kindle is the only mainstream e-reader for which accessibility is actively being addressed.

FilterKeys/Slow Keys: FilterKeys is a utility built into most computer operating systems that provides a pause between pressing a key and the activation of the key's function. This is useful to people who have a tendency to hit keys accidentally; the key will not activate unless it is held down for a specific length of time. The utility is called Slow Keys on Macintosh systems.

hubs: Hubs expand the number of USB ports on a computer so that users can plug in multiple adaptive hardware or peripheral devices, including keyboards, mice, headphones, and scanners.

large print: Print formats that use larger fonts than those used in standard printed materials. Large print is usually defined as using 16 or 18 pt. font sizes; by contrast, standard materials are usually in 10 or 12 pt. fonts.

learning disabled: Generally refers to people with average or above-average intelligence, as measured by standard tests, who have difficulty with reading, writing, mathematics, memory, or other cognitive functions. Compare with COGNITIVELY DISABLED.

low vision: Generally defined as vision loss that cannot be corrected by lenses or medical intervention. Common causes include macular degeneration (loss of central vision), glaucoma (loss of peripheral vision), and cataracts (fuzzy vision).

open source: Open source describes software where both the end product and the programming code are distributed free of charge. Programmers can then modify the code to create and distribute additional free programs.

operating system: The main software that runs a computer. Windows XP, Windows Vista, Windows 7, Macintosh OS X, and Linux are all examples of common operating systems.

optical character recognition (OCR): Software that works in conjunction with a SCANNER to transfer print materials into an electronic format that can be read using some types of assistive technology.

patch: A small piece of software that updates a program by fixing errors, providing new capabilities, enhancing compatibility with other software, or a combination of these. Patches can usually be downloaded for free from the program manufacturer's website.

PDF: Short for "portable document format," PDF is an electronic file format designed to ensure that files look the same to all users regardless of the type of computer they are using. Unfortunately, PDF files are frequently created in a way that makes them difficult or impossible to access by assistive technology users.

People-First Language: A linguistic convention that places a relevant fact about the individual before a mention of his or her disability, for example, "woman with Down syndrome," "doctor who is paraplegic," and "award-winning actor with multiple disabilities." The intention is to avoid defining individuals solely by their physical, sensory, or cognitive capabilities. Many, but not all, people with disabilities favor this convention.

pointer: A visible indicator of where actions will occur if a mouse button is clicked or a key is pressed. As the mouse is moved, the pointer moves correspondingly. Pointers may also be referred to as "cursors."

puffy paint: Also called "fabric paint" or "3D paint," puffy paint can be used to make certain keyboard keys easier for blind people or people with reduced tactile sensitivity to feel.

refreshable braille: A means of translating onscreen information into a BRAILLE format. Refreshable braille devices have pins that move up and down to display braille letters.

repetitive strain injury or **repetitive stress injury (RSI)**: One of several types of injuries to the hand or upper arm. As the name suggests, it can be caused by overuse or improper use not only of keyboards and mice but also of meat cleavers, barber shears, and so forth. Carpal tunnel syndrome is probably the best known type of RSI; others include tendonitis, De Quervain syndrome, and "gamer's thumb."

ribbons: Traditionally, users have activated functions within a software program by selecting them from a pull-down menu. Ribbon interfaces replace menus with a more graphics-based display that may not work with older assistive technologies. Ribbons were introduced as a feature in Microsoft Office 2007 and have since been provided in a few other products.

scanners: Hardware devices that are used to transfer printed materials into a computer-readable format.

scanning: An input method whereby letters or other items on a screen are highlighted sequentially. When the desired item is highlighted, the user clicks a mouse or presses a SWITCH to select it.

screen readers: Software programs designed to provide computer access for people with little or no ability to see a monitor. Screen readers typically include a voice output capability and keyboard commands to substitute for mouse use. Many also include DRIVERS for running REFRESHABLE BRAILLE devices. Compare with TEXT READERS.

Slow Keys: *See* FILTERKEYS.

smartphone: A phone that performs functions far beyond placing and receiving standard phone calls. Smartphones can be used for running APPS, accessing the Internet, sending and receiving e-mail, and a variety of other functions.

StickyKeys: A utility built into most computer operating systems that allows multiple key combinations to be hit sequentially; for example, an asterisk can be generated by pressing the Shift key, releasing it, and then pressing the 8 key.

switches: Switches plug into various types of standard devices, allowing them to be operated more easily by people with severe physical disabilities. Switches can be operated by light pressure, blowing, eyebrow movement, biting, and so forth. They are also useful to some people with cognitive disabilities.

tablet: Portable computers that use a touch screen for input, eliminating the need for standard mouse and keyboard hardware. Most tablets have some level of built-in accessibility, and their ability to run APPS greatly increases their accessibility potential.

text readers: Software programs that read text aloud. These programs are generally most helpful to people with cognitive or learning disabilities or to other sighted people who want auditory help with reading or proofreading; use of a mouse is generally required. Compare with SCREEN READERS.

universal design: A concept promoting product design that meets the needs of as many individuals as possible, regardless of their capabilities, language, culture, or other considerations.

USB: The contemporary standard for plugs on hardware devices such as keyboards and mice, used to attach the device to the computer. USB plugs are distinguished by being flat and rectangular as opposed to older style round plugs.

USB hubs: *See* HUBS.

voice recognition software: Software that can be used to turn spoken words into onscreen text and/or mouse commands. It will not work with all voices or in all environments. Sometimes called "speech recognition," "voice input," or "speech input."

Bibliography

Note: This bibliography is not intended to be exhaustive. If there is a good resource you don't see on this list, please e-mail it to me at jane@janevincent.com, and it will get added to the book's blog at http://www.janevincent.com/iceact.

General Resources on Library Best Practices

In addition to the works referenced within the chapters, the following titles focus on specific relevant topics.

Planning and Budgeting

Carpenter, Julie. 2008. *Library Project Funding*. New York: Neal-Schuman.

Cohn, John M., and Ann L. Kelsey. 2010. *The Complete Library Technology Planner*. New York: Neal-Schuman.

Harriman, Joy H.P. 2008. *Creating Your Library's Business Plan*. New York: Neal-Schuman.

Larson, Jeanette C., and Herman L. Totten. 2008. *The Public Library Policy Writer*. New York: Neal-Schuman.

MacKellar, Pamela H., and Stephanie K. Gerding. 2010. *Winning Grants*. New York: Neal-Schuman.

Collection Development

Chapman, Liz. 2004. *Managing Acquisitions in Library and Information Services, Revised Edition*. New York: Neal-Schuman.

Hibner, Holly, and Mary Kelly. 2010. *Making a Collection Count*. Oxford: Chandos Publishing.

Marketing

Walters, Suzanne. 2004. *Library Marketing That Works!* New York: Neal-Schuman.

Wolfe, Lisa A. 2005. *Library Public Relations, Promotions, and Communications*. New York: Neal-Schuman.

Training

Eng, Sidney. 2010. *Managing Technology and Managing Change in Libraries.* Oxford: Chandos Publishing.

Houghton-Jan, Sarah. 2010. *Technology Training in Libraries.* New York: Neal-Schuman.

Thompson, Susan M., ed. 2008. *Core Technology Competencies for Librarians and Library Staff.* New York: Neal-Schuman.

Todaro, Julie, and Mark L. Smith. 2006. *Training Library Staff and Volunteers to Provide Extraordinary Customer Service.* New York: Neal-Schuman.

Evaluation

Markless, Sharon, and David Streatfield. 2006. *Evaluating the Impact of Your Library.* New York: Neal-Schuman.

General Resources on Disability

The following are good places to look for information on a variety of disability-related topics.

"Cornucopia of Disability Information." State University of New York at Buffalo, http://codi.buffalo.edu/.

Disability.gov, http://www.disability.gov/.

"Disability Resource Index." Disability Resource Directory, http://www.disability-resource.com/disabilityresource.html.

"DRM Guide to Disability Resources on the Internet." Disability Resources Monthly, http://www.disabilityresources.org/.

Resources on Etiquette and Appropriate Language

A significant part of Chapter 5 discusses disability etiquette and appropriate language to use when speaking with or about people with disabilities. Here are some additional useful resources.

Disability Etiquette. United Spinal Association, http://www.unitedspinal.org/pdf/DisabilityEtiquette.pdf.

"Effective Interaction." The Office of Disability Employment Policy (U.S.), http://www.dol.gov/odep/pubs/fact/effectiveinteraction.htm.

Language Guide on Disability. Employment Development Department, State of California, http://www.edd.ca.gov/pdf_pub_ctr/de6031.pdf.

"Talking about Disability." The Memphis Center for Independent Living, http://www.mcil.org/mcil/mcil/talking.htm.

American Library Association Resources

Important Issues. Association of Specialized and Cooperative Library Agencies, http://www.ala.org/ala/mgrps/divs/ascla/asclaissues/issues.cfm.

Library Accessibility: What You Need to Know. Tip sheets. Association of Specialized and Cooperative Library Agencies, http://www.ala.org/ala/mgrps/divs/ascla/asclaprotools/accessibilitytipsheets/.

Serving People with Disabilities, by Rhea Joyce Rubin. American Library Association, http://www.ala.org/ala/aboutala/offices/olos/outreachresource/docs/people_with_disabilities.pdf.

Resources on Web Accessibility

"Section 508 Resource Page." International Center for Disability Resources on the Internet, http://www.icdri.org/section508/index.htm.

"WAI Resources." Web Accessibility Initiative (WAI), http://www.w3.org/WAI/Resources/.

"Web Accessibility, Libraries, and the Law," by Camilla Fulton. Library and Information Technology Association (LITA), http://www.ala.org/ala/mgrps/divs/lita/ital/prepub/fulton.pdf.

WebAIM, http://www.webaim.org/.

Listservs and Discussion Groups

Accessible Libraries Discussion Group, http://www.webjunction.org/801/-/resources/discussion.

Association on Higher Education and Disability, http://www.ahead.org/sigs/technology/resources. Several listservs related to technology and people with disabilities are mentioned. Unfortunately, the two that specifically cover libraries appear to be inactive as of this writing.

Bay Area Disability Services Librarians (BADSL). To subscribe, contact Jane Vincent at jane@janevincent.com.

Disabled Student Services in Higher Education. To subscribe, send an e-mail to LISTSERV@LISTSERV.BUFFALO.EDU, leave the subject field blank, and put the following line in the body of the e-mail: SUBSCRIBE DSSHE-L.

RESNA (an organization of assistive technology professionals). To subscribe, send an e-mail to listserv@maelstrom.stjohns.edu, leave the subject field blank, and put the following line in the body of the e-mail: subscribe resna yourfirstname yourlastname.

Organizations and Conferences Relating to Computers and Disability

Assistive Technology Industry Association (ATIA), http://www.atia.org/. Professional organization of assistive technology developers and providers. Conference held annually at varying times of the year in either Chicago or Orlando.

Closing the Gap (CTG), http://www.closingthegap.com/. Organization focused on computers and disability, particularly in K–12 education. Conference held annually, late October, in Minneapolis.

RESNA (an association for the advancement of rehabilitation technology), http://www.resna.org/. Professional interdisciplinary organization concerned with all aspects of rehabilitation technology; conference features some presentations and equipment displays related to computers; has special interest group on computer applications. Conference held annually, mid-June, in varying locations.

Technology and Persons with Disabilities (CSUN), http://www.csun.edu/cod/. Conference focused on computers and disability, particularly in postsecondary education and employment; sponsored by California State University–Northridge. Conference held annually, mid-March, in San Diego.

Sources of Free Electronic Books

Bookshare (free to qualified students, memberships available to others, proof of disability required to access copyrighted materials), http://www.bookshare.org/.

Online Books Page, University of Pennsylvania (facilitates searching for a specific title or the works of a specific author), http://onlinebooks.library.upenn.edu/.

Project Gutenberg (over 30,000 out-of-copyright texts available for free), http://www.gutenberg.org/.

Resources on Accessible Communication Methods

These provide general tips and should be supplemented by queries to your focus group members and other contacts about their preferences.

"Communication Tips with People Who Are Deaf or Hard of Hearing." e-Michigan Deaf and Hard of Hearing People, http://www.michdhh.org/ hearing/ comm_tips.html.

"Defining PDF Accessibility." WebAIM, http://webaim.org/techniques/acrobat/.

"FAQs and General TTY Etiquette Tips for New TTY Users." Rochester Institute of Technology, http://library.rit.edu/depts/ref/research/deaf/ ttyuse.html.

"A Guide to Making Documents Accessible to People Who Are Blind or Visually Impaired." American Council of the Blind, http://www.acb.org/accessible-formats.html.

"Making Word Documents Accessible." Coastline Community College, http:// www.coastline.edu/departments/specialprograms/page.cfm?LinkID=499.

Resources on Making Meetings/Programs Accessible

Attention should be given to accessibility for any meeting, program, or similar event sponsored by the library; particular attention should be paid if people with disabilities are the prime audience. The following are three good resources on event accessibility.

"Invite, Welcome, and Respect: Planning Accessible Meetings and Events." Washington State Arts Commission, http://www.arts.wa.gov/projects/ documents/Planning-Accessible-Events.pdf.

"Making Accessibility Real: A Guide for Planning Meetings, Conferences, and Gathering." The Home and Community-Based Services Resource Network, http://tcsip.tarjancenter.ucla.edu/docs/HCBSAccessibleMeetings.pdf.

"Removing Barriers: Planning Meetings That Are Accessible to All Participants." North Carolina Office on Disability and Health, http://www.fpg.unc.edu/ ~ncodh/pdfs/rbmeetingguide.pdf.

Index

Braille translation software, 24
Brochures, 88
Browsers, 19, 22, 23, 69
Budgeting, 57–62

C

Cables (for connecting equipment), 44
Calgary (AB, Canada) Public Library,
107–108
California Library Association (CLA), 57
Canadian National Institute for the Blind
(CNIB), 107–108
Captioning, 5
Carpal tunnel syndrome. *See* Repetitive strain
injury
Casing barriers, 42
CCTVs. *See* Closed-circuit televisions
(CCTVs)
CD-ROMs, 42
Census, 2
Chairs. *See* Adjustable chairs
Change Function, 86
Cheat sheets, 94
Checkouts of assistive hardware, 104
Children, 2–3, 29
CLA. *See* California Library Association
(CLA)
Closed-circuit televisions (CCTVs), 45
Cognitive disability
accommodation strategies, 29, 36, 37–42
communication strategies, 5–6
definition, 124
etiquette, 97
Color blindness, 22, 124
Color contrast
as comprehension accommodation, 38,
45
on keyboards, 30, 31
as low vision accommodation, 7
on monitors, 20–21, 22, 23
and websites, 72
Colorado Libraries, 10
Commercial products vs. freeware, 53–54
Communication channels, 83, 88
Communication formats, 5–8, 132
Community partners, 8–10, 51, 61–62,
111
Compatibility. *See* Hardware compatibility;
Software compatibility
Computer literacy, 3
Computer reluctance, 88
Conferences, 51, 131–132
Conflict resolution, 65, 67
Connectors, types, 67–68

Contra Costa County (CA) Library, 56–57
Contrast. *See* Color contrast
Copiers, 55
CPU barriers. *See* Casing barriers
Creative solutions, 19, 32, 37, 41–42
Cursor. *See* Pointer (onscreen)

D

DAISY (file format), 24, 72–73, 124
Data gathering, 4–5
Deafness
accommodation strategies, 6, 28
Deaf vs. deaf, 5, 91, 124
etiquette, 96
Delta Gamma sorority, 9
Demographics, 51, 60
Dewey Decimal System, 85
Dexterity disability, 25–37, 44–45
Dictionaries, 38
Direct selection (onscreen keyboard option),
28
Disability, 2–3, 17, 124, 130
Disability organizations, 9
Disability.gov, 52
Discussion groups, 131
Display settings (Windows operating system), 21,
115
Double-clicking, 34
Dragon NaturallySpeaking, 32
See also Voice recognition software
Drivers, 67, 115, 124
DVDs, 42
Dvorak keyboard layout, 27, 124
Dwell (onscreen keyboard option), 28
Dycem, 32

E

E-books, 72, 124, 132
Educational institutions, 9
Elders
accommodation strategies, 23, 29
appropriate language, 92
as assistive technology users, 2–3, 117
Electronic formats, 8, 41, 71–73
E-mail, 7
Emotional disabilities, 5–6, 97
English as a second language, 3
Environmental model of disability, 17
E-readers, 72–73, 124
Ergonomics, 29, 43
Etiquette, 92–94, 96–97, 130
Evaluation, 102–111
Extended Services library card, 14

About the Author

Jane Vincent holds a Master of Arts in Library Science degree from the University of Michigan. For the past 14 years she has worked for the Center for Accessible Technology (Berkeley, CA), providing consultation to libraries and other agencies on assistive technology acquisition and use throughout California, as well as evaluating website accessibility for businesses and organizations and performing assistive technology evaluations with individuals. Jane has presented at the Public Library Association conference as well as at multiple conferences on assistive technology, aging, and usability. She has provided several trainings on various assistive technology topics for Infopeople, the training arm of the California State Library. She was a primary contributor to *Access on Main Street* (http://www.accessonmainstreet.net/), a unique blog tracking the implementation of assistive technology features in mainstream products. Her writings have also been published in *Library Hi-Tech News* (special issue editor), *JASIS*, *Communication Disorders Quarterly*, and *MacWorld*.